Kiddie Patter
and
Little Feats

Samuel Patrick Smith

Kiddie Patter
and
Little Feats

How to Entertain
Pre-schoolers
with
Magic
and
Funny Stuff

SPS Publications

Post Office Box 769 • Tavares, Florida 32778

Also by Samuel Patrick Smith

Booking Yourself: How to Do It Successfully (audio)
Make It Happen: New Ideas on Booking Yourself (audio)
The Professional Entertainer's Album (audio)
Sell Your Act with Posters!
Sell Your Act with Letters!
Sell Your Act with Letters! (audio)
Sell Your Act with Brochures and Flyers!
Big Laughs for Little People
On Stage!
Advice from a Pro...On Playing Shows (editor)
The Edison of Magic (editor)

Disclaimer

This publication is designed to provide accurate and authoritative information in regard to the subject matter covered. It is sold with the understanding that the publisher is not engaged in rendering legal, accounting, or other professional services. If legal advice or other expert assistance is required, the services of a competent professional should be sought. The purpose of this publication is to educate and entertain. The author and publisher shall have neither liability nor responsibility to any person or entity with respect to any loss or damage caused or alleged to be caused directly or indirectly by the information contained herein.

KIDDIE PATTER AND LITTLE FEATS

Printed in the United States of America

Dedication

To my father,
Gene Nelson Smith

*T*his is an unusual picture of my father, because he appears to be relaxing—doing nothing! The truth is that he is one of the most industrious men I know, and he managed to instill his work ethic into his children. (Some of us are still trying to overcome it!) Somehow, he found time to take me to magic club meetings, build me a Vanishing Head illusion and a Super-X suspension, and buy me a subscription to *Genii* magazine! He's still waiting on the trip around the world I promised him. So, Dad, thanks for all the help, but most of all, thanks for a good example. I'm proud of your accomplishments, and especially proud of you!

Acknowledgments

There are certain influential people who could be mentioned in the acknowledgments of any book I produce, who may not have directly contributed to the writing. And particularly in this volume of magic for pre-school children, I think of those who have supported and encouraged me since my own pre-school days! For instance, my parents, my grandparents, my brother Lee, and my sister Cheryl were early childhood influences who likely helped shape my sense of humor and manner of dealing with children.

Then there was Miss Mita, my pre-school babysitter, a grandma-figure. And Mrs. Cross, my nursery school teacher who showed us how to entertain ourselves without a television, VCR, or video games. Later came a year at Bluebird Nursery School in Mount Dora.

And of course, my friends of that period, Michael Straub and Amy Vanzant, were important influences. (Amy and I went through nursery school, kindergarten, 12 grades of public school, and college together!) I know Sigmund Freud liked people to delve into their childhood to discover the roots of all their problems—but I enjoyed being a little kid! Sorry, Sigmund!

Specifically in the writing of this book, I want to thank my wife Laurel who handled many details of our business while I was busily typing on the computer.

Also, my sister Cheryl was a great help, editing and helping me come up with a title. Several years ago when I was trying to find a title for a newly written manuscript, Cheryl and I jointly engineered *Big Laughs for Little People*.

At the same time, we came up with the title for this present book which was then only roughly outlined. It worked something like this—

CHERYL: How about, *The Pitter Patter of Little Feats*, f–e–a–t–s?

SAMMY: Or maybe, *Booking Yourself with Little Feats.*

CHERYL: [Silence.]

SAMMY: *Make It Happen with Pitter Patter?*

CHERYL: Next.

SAMMY: *Sell Your Act with Little Feats?*

CHERYL: *Beating a Dead Horse?*

SAMMY: Okay, okay. How about, *The Kiddie Patter of Little Feats.*

CHERYL: Or, *Kiddie Patter and Little Feats.*

And there it was!

Another helpful person was David Ginn. He read the manuscript, offered suggestions, and encouraged me. Come to think of it, he does that with every book I write! Thanks, David!

My good friend Fetaque Sanders passed away before this book was finished, but I talked to him at length and read him portions of the manuscript while he was in the hospital unable to talk. He later made a brief recovery (we had a final visit in person a few weeks before he died) and we talked on the phone about some of this material. Fetaque was great. He saw me present all of the routines in this book, some of them many times, as he accompanied me to shows in the Nashville area during a seven-year period.

While Fetaque had a two-and-a-half month stay in the

hospital, Scott Humston arranged my lodging in Nashville on two occasions so I could see Fetaque and work on the book between hospital visits. Scott also read some of the early chapters, said he liked them, and wanted to see more. So, Scott, here it is!

Then there were those who helped edit this book and didn't even know it: the audiences who came to my lectures while the book was in progress. Although the lecture was based on my first book of children's magic, *Big Laughs for Little People*, I began including explanations of how to deal with the very young. I was able to see when my rationale for a particular handling of an effect made sense to people, and when it needed more explanation. So while Laurel and I lectured in Victoria, BC; Vancouver, BC; Tacoma, WA; Portland, OR; Albany, OR; Boston; Albany, NY; Ithaca, NY; North Haven, CT; Harrisburg, PA; Baltimore, MD, Wilmington, DE; Canton, OH; and other places, I had the manuscript with me and the wheels were turning.

For the photographs, I turned to Martha Martin of Leesburg, Florida, who illustrated *Big Laughs for Little People*. Brittany Birch and Reagan Lynn were my models and were great to work with. Thanks, Brittany and Reagan! And thanks to Greg McMahon for his work on the book cover, and to my able proofreaders: Brenda Hahne, Cheryl Ritchie, and Laurel Smith.

Some other people who deserve a large share of the credit for *Kiddie Patter and Little Feats* are the pre-school and kindergarten directors who started booking me in 1979. While other magicians were scrambling for birthday parties, I found a completely untapped market in pre-schools. I was amazed that I had *no competition*. Although I have performed for a wide variety of audiences over the years, the sheer *quantity* of performances I did for young audiences removed a lot of the rough edges from my presentations.

Many influences have led to the production of this book and to the development of the philosophy behind it. I am grateful for each one. Most of all, I want to thank God for giving me a wonderful family, the perfect wife, and a life so good—even with its problems and temporary limitations— that I wouldn't trade places with *anyone*.

Contents

Introducing
Kiddie Patter
and
Little Feats

We are not sent into this world to do anything into which we cannot put our hearts. We have certain work to do for our bread, and that is to be done strenuously; other work to do for our delight, and that is to be done heartily; neither is to be done by halves or shifts, but with a will; and what is not worth this effort is not to be done at all.

–John Ruskin

Introduction

Ten years ago, I graduated from college—not Magna Cum Laude, but Thank the Lawdy. With my diploma in hand, it occurred to me that I should cast about for a way to earn an honest living. Not wanting the inconvenience of a nine-to-five job, I embarked on a career in magic.

One of my first shows that year was at a child care center in Tampa, Florida. The show was scheduled for afternoon, so children of all ages would be present.

I stood outside the door to a large room where the inmates awaited. Actually, they weren't waiting—the fun had already begun. I could hear the children inside screaming and running around the room. I could also hear teachers trying to calm the mob before introducing me.

Finally, I was summoned. I stepped into the room. The noise level was even greater than I had realized. The woman "in charge" managed to threaten the children down to a low roar while she told them that the magician was about to start the show. A momentary lull in the babble came like calm before the storm. I stepped forward and the pandemonium continued.

I began my show anyway, though I barely could hear my own voice. At first I was angry, but I soon discovered that three or four kids on the front row were watching and seemed to hear what I was saying. So I decided to do the show in good cheer—for those kids down front. And I did just that.

When the show was over, I packed my props and dashed for the nearest exit. I made it outside where I found the woman with my check. "Thank you so much," she gushed, "thank you."

And then to my complete surprise and utter confusion, she said, "You have such a wonderful way with children!"

A hundred kids in that room had no conception of what I had done; I doubt if they realized I was even in the room.

I drove home wondering if I should stay in the business. I thought of the raging crowd of children not paying as much attention to me as they had given to the proof-of-purchase seal on their box of cereal that morning.

But then I thought about the front row of kids, and about that teacher. "You have such a wonderful way with children." It was amazing that she could say such a thing, but I decided not to quit.

As the months went by, my bookings increased, and so did my experience. Gradually, I learned the tricks of the trade—how to deal with different ages of children, how to entertain school-age kids, and how to appeal to pre-schoolers. After I reached the point of doing almost 450 shows a year, I decided to reduce my show schedule to a more reasonable 200 to 300. With the balance of my time, I would write what I had learned about entertaining children.

And so, in 1990, I wrote and published *Big Laughs for Little People*. The generous response to that book, and to my lecture tour based on the book, encouraged me to continue. Amid the roar of a busy schedule, I like to pretend that someone is saying, "You have such a wonderful way with books!" And so, here I am again!

This new book is designed to help performers think about the special interests and needs of pre-school audiences.

Whether you are performing for a kindergarten class or a birthday party, these principles and routines will work. They *have* worked and continue to work for me.

Sometimes I hear people say, "You can't do a magic show for four- and five-year-olds. They don't understand magic— to them, everything is possible, so *nothing* is magic." I can only say that this belief is not based on reality. The fact is, very young children can be fooled, do appreciate magic, and enjoy watching magic shows. I know, because I've given thousands of performances for these little folks, and they have returned many delightful moments.

For instance, I remember

. . . the time when a genuinely enthusiastic four-year-old called out in response to a trick which had fooled him, "That's a *good one,* Sammy!"

. . . the time I asked for "the quietest person in the room," and a completely sincere five-year-old leapt to his feet, calling out loudly, "That's *me!* I'm a *very* quiet person!"

. . . the time when a group a pre-schoolers were talking to me after a show, each one telling me about their new toys and clothes they got for Christmas. "I have a new Barbie." "I have a train set." But one little tyke pushed his way close to me, took hold of my arm, and said, "I have a buddy."

They have certainly been a pleasure to entertain. And looking back on some of the many rewarding moments, I'd like to say to those pre-schoolers, "You have such a wonderful way with magicians!"

*Those
who bring sunshine
into the lives of others
cannot keep it from
themselves.*

–Sir James M. Barrie

The Customer Is Always Right

or

How to Amuse the Little Ones

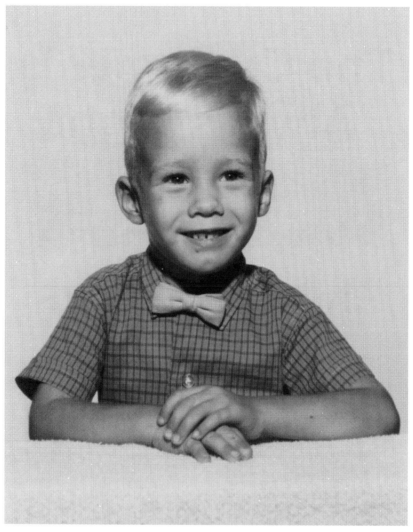

My authority for writing a book about pre-schoolers comes from personal experience: I was one!

Can the Magician
Come Out and Play Today?

To be successful in any line of work, you have to discover what your customers want, then adapt your services to meet their needs. Entertaining pre-school children is no exception. If a performer learns what appeals to the little ones and adapts his or her act to their tastes, success waits just around the corner!

The pleasant thing about pre-schoolers is that they don't have to be dazzled with a glitzy revue—their tastes are relatively pure, and they haven't become calloused from excessive exposure to entertainment. Later in life, children sometimes feel as though they have seen it all. Nothing you could show them would satisfy their cynical expectations— in short, they are ripe to the point of fermentation (spoiled). But take heart, because many children will grow out of this stage and actually turn out to be respectable citizens. However, at the tender ages of three, four, and five, most children have not yet entered their skeptical years. Their tastes are still simple.

Do you remember a time when you were very young and were given a simple toy to play with which kept you fascinated for hours? I remember my dear old nursery school teacher, Mrs. Cross, who gave us paint brushes and cans of water and let us express our artistic best on her sidewalk. Painting with water is a very temporary art form, but most of the art wasn't very good anyway! But the *entertainment value* of those simple props kept a four-year-old Sammy Smith happy for a long time. Likewise, your props can be simple and your show can be easy to do—but you must use those props and present your show according to the old maxim, "The customer is always right." Your performance must strike the funny bone of the children, it must capture their imagination, and keep their interest. To help you achieve those seemingly lofty aims, I have developed the following list of things which amuse and delight young children.

Different Strokes for Little Folks

(1) **Pre-schoolers love stories.** Come to think of it, almost everyone loves stories! Stories get us involved with the characters and let us imagine ourselves as part of the adventure without the effort of actually being there. Pre-schoolers, in particular, want to be free to use their imaginations. They may hesitate to come up "on stage" to assist you, but they still want to be involved. So whenever your patter can be delivered in the form of a good story, the little ones will literally lean forward in anticipation.

Interestingly, it doesn't seem to matter how many times they have already heard the story. Sometimes after I complete a routine with a story patter-line, a child in the audience will say, "Let's hear it again!" They are used to hearing bedtime stories repeated, and now with the variety of toys which play cassette tapes, children often plug in Mother Goose and listen to the story of the Ugly Duckling for the tenth or twentieth time.

(2) **Pre-schoolers enjoy repetition.** When you bring out your favorite prop, a fourth grader may say with disdain,

"I've seen *that* before." A pre-schooler may say much the same thing, but with different emphasis: "Oh! I've seen that before!" And then, bless his pre-school heart, he will add, "Let's see it again!" This trait of a young child gives you more latitude when you play repeat engagements. I never do the same show two times in a row, but I sometimes get such questions as, "Did you bring Alice the Alligator this time?"

I reply, "No—I brought another friend I think you'll really like to meet, but when I get home, I'll tell Alice that you asked about her!" A year later, I may be able to repeat many of the routines with only minor adjustments. So Alice the Alligator or Rocky the Rockin' Raccoon may safely return to the stage.

(3) **Pre-schoolers like to share their knowledge.** They are learning so many new things at this young age, that they are excited and anxious to tell you about them. This is why you can easily work in safety messages or good behavior points into your routines. You allow the children to tell you the message.

For instance, you may show a flower and say, "I like flowers because they smell so good. But you know, we should never put these in our mouths because, some flowers can be—" At this point, you trail off and let the children say back to you, "Poisonous." You continue. "That's right. So even though they smell very good, we never put them into our—" And the children complete the sentence, "Mouths." Let them be smart and show off their knowledge. It makes them feel good about themselves to reveal some of their learning, and it makes them like *you* all the more for being smart enough to realize how smart *they* are!

(4) **Pre-schoolers appreciate gentleness.** If you have ever watched Fred Rogers work with a group of children on *Mr. Rogers' Neighborhood,* you will see a genius of gentleness at work. I know that style of talking will disgust the average ten-year-old, but Mr. Rogers is talking to four-year-olds. They appreciate the easy-going, soft-spoken approach. Think of other children's entertainers or celebrities who appeal to the very young: Captain Kangaroo is a good example. His kind manner always appealed to me when I was in kindergarten. Somehow, it lured me into the show, making me feel comfortable and comforted. Young children do not understand sarcasm, do not like brusqueness, and are afraid of loud, brash people. Even if your personality is the antithesis of Fred Rogers, keep your voice on the soft side and your manner kind and warm to appeal to small children.

(5) **Children like puppets.** This may stem from their close association with dolls and stuffed animals. Whatever the reason, children laugh at the antics of puppets and become quite sympathetic with any character who is sad or in trouble. They naturally want the puppets to come out on top and be the winners. I often include a simple puppet routine in my shows for pre-schoolers—and the kids remember them and ask about the characters for a long time.

You don't have to use ventriloquism to do a delightful routine with a puppet. The puppet can whisper things into your ear which you then relate to the audience. For instance, you may say to a rabbit puppet: "Puff, are you going to show these nice people a magic trick?" Puff shakes his head *no.*

You say, "You're not?! Why not?" The rabbit leans over and whispers in your ear.

Magic times at the library delight children of all ages

By LIZA SWENN MARTIN
New Volusian correspondent

The blond, bespectacled countenance of Sammy Smith has become a familiar one to children (and adults) attending the Florida Summer Library Programs in Volusia County over the last five years. Sammy Smith the Magician, delights the young and the not-so-young with his corny jokes and light humor.

His repertoire includes a variety of "magic critters," including a rabbit puppet named Puff; a snake that emerges from, where else, a tennis ball can; a fish family; and a very thin chicken. Among some of the best-loved tricks Sammy performs are producing an egg from an empty bag and making money appear from a child's ear.

Sammy Smith has been performing magic tricks since he was 8 years old, with a great-uncle helping and encouraging. In college, he majored in journalism, performing his magic at parties when not in class. Upon graduation he went into magic fulltime.

In addition to "playing the library circuit" during the summer months, he performs his act at schools and day care centers. He also has been traveling the lecture route for the last year-and-a-half, speaking to magic clubs and conventions in 20 states from Washington to New York. His topic: "Big Laughs for Little People: How to Entertain Children with Magic and Comedy," the same title as one of his five published books.

You look at the audience and relate the answer: "He doesn't feel like it."

Turning to the puppet, you ask, "Do you feel like seeing the 'Sawing-a-Rabbit-in-Half Trick'?"

The puppet vigorously shakes his head *no*, then whispers in your ear.

"You don't like to split hares?" The children laugh because the rabbit is giving you a hard time, and the adults will laugh and groan at the joke.

(6) **Children love rabbits.** You will hear screams of delight when you produce a rabbit, but if you try to force little kids to pet the rabbit or get too close too fast, you will also hear screams of terror! They love rabbits—that is, they love to look at them and, in their own good time, touch their soft fur. But the uncertain movements of a live rabbit can cause apprehension in some children. (Likewise, the uncertain movements of children can cause apprehension in some rabbits!)

The good news is that you may be able to get away with using a fake rabbit. Sometimes after performing my routine with Puff the Rabbit (a rabbit-in-the-hat hand puppet, named after a real rabbit I once knew), small children will ask, "Is he real?" The puppet, to an adult, is obviously just that: a hand puppet. It doesn't look realistic and isn't intended to be anything other than a puppet. But small children haven't had enough experiences with live animals and puppets to tell the difference, provided the puppet is life-sized. If children can believe that a hand puppet is real, then a little practice with a realistic spring rabbit will certainly convince them.

If you are using a spring animal, it isn't necessary to say whether he is real or artificial. When I do a routine with a spring raccoon, children (even elementary-age) will ask if he is real. For the amusement of the adults, I'll often remark, "Yes," and then in undertones add, "in a former life." Or, I sometimes reply, "He's the *realest* raccoon *I've* ever had!"

Taking Stock of Livestock

Since the question of using a rabbit in children's shows comes up frequently, let's discuss the special problems of using animals in programs for pre-schoolers.

For six years I featured a live rabbit in my shows, Puff the Magic Rabbit—he was a terrific hit. He was so friendly, he would patiently let 30 or 40 children pet him, one by one. He was the nicest rabbit I ever met. But for the performer on the road, using a rabbit in the show can present difficulties. For one, here in Florida, I was unable to use him in the show during the warmer months, from June through September.

Puff the Magic Rabbit relaxes in his luxury condo in Tavares, Florida. Puff was a featured part of my show for six years. 1989 photo.

Transporting a rabbit in a hot car is no good for the rabbit or for the magician's conscience. And even during cooler months, I found I was suffering from rabbit anxiety. When I went into a restaurant to eat lunch, I would think, "I wonder how the rabbit is? Is he too hot?" Restaurants don't look kindly on patrons who bring rabbits in with them, though I have wondered if waitresses would make an exception at the International House of Pancakes. You know, *IHOP!*

There is also the issue of personal liability if the rabbit were to bite or scratch a child. Of course, if you don't allow them to pet the rabbit, you avoid that problem and also protect the rabbit from child-abuse. Innocent pre-schoolers may grab his ears or poke at his eyes. For that reason, I always gave a brief but serious lecture if the children were to pet Puff.

I would say, "How many of you would like to have a chance to pet Puff the Magic Rabbit? Okay! In just a few minutes I'm going to give *anyone who wants to pet him* a chance to do that. But if you don't want to touch him, that's okay, too—you can just keep your seat until the others are finished. But before I let you pet Puff the Rabbit, there are a couple very important things we need to remember. First of all, look up here at Puff's ears. These are *long* ears, aren't they?! They are also very sensitive, which means that if you try to pull on his ears, it will hurt him. So if I let you pet Puff the Rabbit, do you promise *not to touch his ears?* Say, 'I promise.' Great!

"Here is another important thing to remember about Puff the Rabbit. Do you see these eye balls? He has big eyes, doesn't he? And did you know that if you try to touch his eyes

"When you're a big celebrity," Puff once told me, "sometimes you've just got to get away from your fans." Here, Puff hides under our 1927 Edison phonograph, evading anxious crowds of paw-print seekers.

or poke at them, that could hurt him, too. It would be just like having *your* eyes poked—you wouldn't like *that* would you? So if I let you pet Puff the Rabbit, do you promise not to touch his eyes? Say, 'I promise.' Okay, that's great.

"Now, there is one last thing I have to tell you about Puff. Do you see this cute little rabbit mouth? That's a very funny-looking mouth, but inside that mouth, Puff has—that's right, *teeth*. And they are sharp teeth. Now Puff would never try to bite someone on purpose. He is a very nice rabbit. *But* if you poked at his mouth, he might think your finger is a carrot and take a great big bite! So promise me one last thing. Promise that you won't try to touch his mouth. Promise? Great!

"When it is your time to come up and say *hi* to Puff, your teacher will tell you. Please wait with your class and keep your seat until your teacher calls you, okay?"

Then as the children came up to see the rabbit, they were instructed to gently pat his head or lightly stroke his back.

In six years, I never had any problems with either the rabbit or a child getting hurt. But since Puff's untimely demise (from natural causes) in 1989, I have had time to think objectively about rabbits in general and about rabbits in magic shows in particular. As a result of this rabbitual contemplation, I have formulated *a startling theory* on livestock.

Sammy's Rabbit Theory

To many children's entertainers, my rabbit theory may seem disrespectful and unfeeling, but here it is: *You don't need a rabbit.* And before you have time to catch your breath, let me offer a shocking corollary to my theory: Not only do you *not* need a rabbit, but using a rabbit in your show may dilute the children's memories of *you.* That's right—that's what I said. Without begrudging the rabbit his fair share of fame and glory, I would rather have the children remember *me, the magic show, and the funny things I did.*

Think about it: The magic show is coming to a close. The children have laughed, been surprised, and had a good time. They have come to trust you, the performer. And now, in a few minutes, this magic show experience will be over. If you close the show saying good-bye to them and having them say their reluctant good-byes to you, what is the last thing they remember? It's the bittersweet farewell to you, the nice magic person.

By contrast, consider what happens when the show ends with the production and petting of a live rabbit: The children go berserk. The rabbit has arrived, and who cares about the

If you're going to use a rabbit, at least get a neat carrying case like this one! I took this picture of Bruce "Sparkles" Johnson and David Ginn at David's home in Atlanta, January 13, 1989. (You can read about the Bunny Barn in David's book, Nearly Unpublished, *published later that year).*

It may be proved with much certainty, that God intends no man to live in this world without working; but it seems no less evident that He intends every man to be happy in his work. It was written: "In the sweat of thy brow," but it was never written: "In the breaking of thy heart."

–John Ruskin

magic person holding the rabbit—just let me see that bunny! What is the last thing they remember about the show? They remember they saw a rabbit and got to touch it! And somewhere in the background of that experience lurks a magician and a show.

If this theory sounds crass and commercialized, it is intended to be! I am looking at my impact as a performer from a commercial viewpoint. A similar situation would be trying to upstage Santa Claus. And if you have ever had Santa Claus walk into a room where you are doing a show, need I say more about the futility of continuing your act?

So there you have it—my theory on the use of rabbits in magic shows. But if you catch me ignoring my own advice sometime, it doesn't mean I've abandoned my theory. It just means that I like rabbits more than I like theories!

Tricks Are for Kids, But Which Tricks?

Presenting a great show for pre-school children begins with selecting the right material. The following two sections suggest the type of effects which appeal to the very young, and the type of material they dislike. I will mention specific effects to illustrate a point, but understanding the psychology of a small child is more important than which tricks you perform.

(1) **Straight-forward magic.** By this, I mean routines which are easy to follow. A child should be able to tell his mommy what he saw. For instance, "That magic lady made a coin disappear." (The actual quotation would be, "That

Here I am with a group of pre-schoolers on November 6, 1987. The picture was taken by Laurel, my bride of three weeks. Note the table with a dragon design: I later got rid of this when some small children were frightened by it. Nowadays, I prefer more cheerful-looking tables.

magic lady made a big penny jistappear!") The important point is that the child understood what happened. If the trick is too complicated, he may not be able to describe it—and he may not even know what happened!

Routines are inappropriate for children if they require too much "set-up" before the climax of the magic. Even as an adult, I have been confused by magicians performing routines with poker hands or tricks which involve counting how many cards are in a stack. If long set-ups confuse an adult, four-year-olds aren't going to follow them well either!

While these children may be very intelligent, their sense of reasoning is not fully developed. So any effect which they can plainly see, and which they can understand without having to reason things out too much, is desirable.

(2) **Colorful effects.** Bright silk scarves, feather flowers, and colorful puppets are all very attractive to three-, four-, and five-year-olds. Such tricks as Blow-Tie (or The Crystal Tube manufactured by Tenyo) and 20th Century Silks are not only good magic effects for any age, but they are bright, colorful, and lightweight. How convenient! And Trevor Lewis' Blooming Bouquet routine is a delightful bit of nonsense which really grabs the attention of pre-schoolers.

Take a trip to a toy store and see what is on display for pre-school children. You will find bright, basic colors, and fun-looking toys. Colors automatically attract small children. Take advantage of this natural inclination and use bright, colorful magic in your show.

(3) **Tricks involving animal characters.** Such effects as Hoppy the Frog, Sammy the Seal, Farmyard Frolics, and Fraidy Cat Rabbit are very effective. The animals can be presented to the children as named characters: "I'd like you to meet Hoppy the Frog. Everybody, say hello to Hoppy." Children like animals, especially pretend animals which seem completely non-threatening to them.

Supreme Magic once produced an effect called The Piggery, based on a little story about five pigs. It wasn't much of a *magic* trick, but the entertainment value was tremendous. The silk-screened pictures of the pigs were very appealing to pre-schoolers, and the names suggested for the pigs were very funny to the kids. The pigs' names were Grunt, Snort, Gobble, Bubble, and—the trouble-maker—Squeak. This was a wonderful example of good magic for pre-schoolers: an animal trick, using bright, colorful pictures, and silly names for the characters.

(4) **Magic with Objects They Recognize.** Children like tricks with crayons, for instance, because they use crayons almost daily. They also like tricks with objects their mothers use around the house—Soft Soap is a good effect, because most children have seen their parents doing laundry.

This principle of doing magic with objects children are familiar with is one reason tricks using balls are particularly good. Strat-O-Spheres, juggling routines, and even Multiplying Billiard Balls all appeal to them, because most children have in their toy box several rubber and plastic balls.

When magicians find out that I do a Billiard Ball routine for children, they are frequently surprised. I've even had magicians tell me all the reasons they would *never* use that effect for kids. Children, they say, don't care about tricks requiring skill—they get bored easily, etc.

But that's exactly why the Billiard Ball routine works— they don't care about the skill, but *they like the prop* itself. "Here, catch this ball." And the ball disappears, and the kids are surprised and delighted, especially when it reappears without your knowledge.

Five Big No-Nos

(1) **No fire effects.** Don't even use flash paper in a dove pan. Fire may frighten some of the children, and it will frighten some of the adults even more! One pre-school director told me that she would *never* have a certain magician back to her school. Why? Because he did an effect with fire—after she

Kindergartener Kendall drew this picture of me performing the Multiplying Billiard Balls. I think this is evidence that tricks with simple props—things kids can relate to—are the most memorable for pre-schoolers.

specifically asked him *not* to use any tricks with blades or flames! The baffling part of the act was not the fire trick—it was the astounding stupidity of the performer proceeding as he wished, against the reasonable request of the customer.

In my *Snake Cake Bake* routine (described in *Big Laughs for Little People*, available for $27 postpaid from your favorite dealer or direct from the publisher, thank you very much), there is one point where a flash of fire in a dove pan would add a showy touch. But I don't do it. Instead, I pretend to light a match and *pretend* to have flames leaping out of the pan. And I let all of the children pretend with me! I make a whooshing noise and a crackling sound like fire, and I gesture with my hands to show the flames. "Look at those flames," I exclaim, "Look at them leaping up high into the air!"

Then I ask in an affirmative tone of voice, "Do you see them?" If the child helper is caught up in the excitement of the trick, she will sometimes say, "Yes!"

I pause, look toward the audience (with the adults in mind) and remark, "This is a better trick than even *I* imagined."

So you can find ways to get around using real fire, even though, in our magician-ish minds, a touch of flame would be dramatic.

(2) **No tricks which appear to be dangerous.** This means no chopper effects: head choppers, arm choppers, finger choppers—who came up with all these mutilation effects anyway? And even such mild stunts as the Sword through Neck—which I personally like and use in my school

show for elementary audiences—should not be performed for pre-schoolers.

Also, effects which appear to use other dangerous items, such as firecrackers or rat traps, should be avoided. Once at a party for five-year-olds, I began a routine with the Ching Soo Firecracker, and quickly ended it when I saw most of the audience shrinking away in genuine fear. I had not lit a fuse or made a big fuss about the firecracker, but those children knew that fireworks can be dangerous. Not being able to distinguish between the real McCoy and artificial McCoys, they were afraid. I dropped the trick and went on to milder magic.

Similarly, you should eliminate effects with needles, razor blades, or knives. Children and teachers do not like them.

(3) **No candy productions without permission.** And I mean the permission of the adults, not the children! If the birthday mom or supervising adult requests that you produce their own candy to distribute, you may choose to do that, using a dove pan or Crystal Silk Cylinder or other production device. But my preference is not to give pre-schoolers candy under any conditions. In their excitement about the show, they would not be as cautious about chewing it as they should be. A child could inadvertantly spit the candy onto a brand-new carpet—or, infinitely worse, a child could choke. Another dangerous scenerio could result from a squabble over who's got whose candy. I simply prefer not to get involved in feeding candy to small children.

(4) **No tricks requiring reading skills.** That is, reading skills on the part of the audience. A seemingly obvious

Simplify, simplify.

–Henry David Thoreau

Simplify.

–Samuel Patrick Smith

point, but one which has been overlooked by some performers trying to do the Eye Chart trick in a "Reading Is Magic" show for four-year-olds! If the crux of a gag depends on a child's successfully reading, "I Can't See A Thing" aloud, the child has to be a *very* competent reader.

In fact, using Supreme's Eye Chart trick in elementary schools, I had to be careful to select no one younger than second grade, and even then I cued the volunteer to say the right thing. Even if a child has some reading skills, he is often under too much stress on stage to read the line clearly. He is likely to say, "I cannot see anything!"

One exception to this rule was my use of Supreme's ABC Stung, where the punchline is the word *stung* on the back of a card. Pre-schoolers couldn't read the word. But as I turned the card over, I said, "You don't want to get—"

I would then point to the word and underline it with my finger. After that brief pause, I would complete my sentence by reading the word *stung* aloud for them.

(5) **No loud noises.** Again, the scare-factor is involved. At birth, children are afraid of two things: falling and loud noises. Flash-bang wands, cap guns, and loud voices tend to put children on edge. In the routine, *Seymour the Seal*, described later in this book, I will show how and why I am able to ignore this rule briefly.

Keep It Simple

Finally, it should go without saying that any effect using cigarettes or playing cards would be inappropriate and ineffective, and complicated tricks involving mathematics

Children of all ages come to public shows. If pre-schoolers are a part of an audience, it's best not to do any tricks which appear to be dangerous or frightening. Such tricks may scare the little ones and will be certain to alarm their parents! Do a show they can all enjoy. Photo by Mary Frank.

or abstract notions will fail to amuse.

I'll never forget doing a show for a church group one Christmas, where young people of all ages were invited. The age-range went from pre-schoolers up to high school students! I was attempting to tie a Christian message to one of the effects when a four- or five-year-old raised his hand. I was curious about what he wanted, so I said, "Yes—what would you like?"

The little boy stood up. The entire audience looked at him expectantly. Then, in a loud, clear voice, the little fellow said, "Mister, I don't understand a thing you're saying." That brought down the house! I finished the trick as well as I could and carried on with the rest of the program, trying to keep things simple.

Big Laughs for Little Laughers

Pre-schoolers have a predictable sense of humor. That's a great advantage, because you can confidently present the same material for virtually any group of young children and count on the same response. Here are four things which tickle the funny bones of pre-schoolers.

(1) **Simple slapstick.** The magician gets bonked on the nose. That's funny. A puppet alligator opens its jaws and scares the grown-up. That's funny, too. It is no longer funny, however, if the children think you have *really* been badly hurt. It's only funny to them as long as they know you're just *playing*.

(2) **Funny names.** Playful-sounding words and names appeal to children: kangaroo, bow-wow, ballooney, muffet,

itsy-bitsy, teeny-weeny, Zaney Blaney, Ickle Pickle, and so forth. One of my own silly words is Hoozleheimer. A child may say, "Do you know what my name is?"

I say, "Yes, of course, you're Hoozleheimer."

The child will laugh and say, "No, you silly, my name is Rebekah."

To which I will reply, "Why, yes, of course. You're Rebekah Hoozleheimer!" More laughter and protests.

I realize how completely ridiculous this looks in print. But to get a better grasp of word-inventions, get a recorded edition of Lewis Carroll's *Through the Looking Glass*. You will hear a wealth of wonderful words. You may not use any of them, but a good recording of the book will stimulate your imagination. You'll begin to see the kinds of words and sounds which appeal to children.

(3) **Silly-looking objects.** Those giant eye-glasses with big, bushy eye brows and a great big nose strike pre-schoolers as very funny. It's also a great laughing matter for you to bring out giant sized props—a huge pair of scissors, an over-sized tooth, a big sandwich, or a hat that's far too big.

(4) **Costumes.** Costumes which amuse children are the fairly simple ones—basic colors and basic concepts work best. (Scary costumes aren't funny.) The most comical situations include costumes which you put on *in front of the children,* such as—the magician dresses up as an elf.

Of course, it is always great fun to dress up a child volunteer. David Ginn has documented this well in his many books and video tapes. But keep in mind that pre-schoolers are more hesitant than elementary students to put on costumes. You can't just snatch a kid out of the audience and

For good examples of the kind of nonsensical talk children like, turn to Lewis Carroll's Through the Looking Glass. *(Here, Alice is conversing with Tweedledum and Tweedledee.) A recording of the book will be especially useful as you are able to hear the cadence of the words.*

expect him or her to wear a great big hat, a coat, and hold a magic wand. You must first earn the trust of the child by having her on stage for a few minutes and building up to the job of wearing a certain hat. You can say, "Now, Lynne, I don't let *everybody* wear this hat. But I'm going to let *you* wear it, because you're my friend."

There are times, of course, when you can tell that a child is confident, comfortable, and cooperative to begin with— you have already earned his trust, or he is just a confident kid. Then you can be less cautious about loading him up with a silly costume.

You also may find a naughty rascal who won't cooperate. He may take your costume and throw it on the ground in defiance. If I discover this rebellious spirit in a helper, I will often say, "Well, David, to make this trick work, my magic helper has to wear this hat. Thanks for coming up to help, but you may have your seat now." And I usher the boy back into the audience and find a more rational assistant.

It is important to distinguish between an uncooperative attitude and mere shyness. If a costume-wearer is just extremely bashful but does not mind staying on stage, I may volunteer to wear the outfit myself and let the tender little tot tarry for the trick. I accept shyness but not naughtiness. After working with young children for a while, you can usually tell the difference.

Getting Them to Respond

If you have ever performed for children, you already know that the best applause you'll hear is their laughter, and the finest standing ovation you'll receive is the look of sheer glee on their faces. Most children have not yet learned the manners and mannerisms of theater-goers. But that doesn't mean you can't get them to respond by clapping and laughing at the right places. It simply means that it is your job to teach them.

The principal way that pre-schoolers know when to react is by watching your facial cues. For instance, a blue silk handkerchief suddenly appears in a clear, plastic box. You look at the box and silk with a blank expression for a moment. Then you look at the children with a *well-what-do-*

you-know-about-that! expression. That's their cue that something unusual has happened. Of course, they *already know* that the silk handkerchief shouldn't be in the little box, but your look of "how about that" gives them permission to react. It reassures them that they were right in the first place— something funny *has* happened.

Beware of using the same facial expression too many times in the same show. Your facial cue loses impact if the children become accustomed to it. Vary your reactions. Here are a few of the more useful expressions to choose from:

• **Well, what do you know about that!** As mentioned above, this tells the children that the magic has happened.

• **I can't believe it!** A more astounded expression to indicate something *really wonderful* has taken place.

• **That scared me!** They laugh if they think you are scared, but not *too* scared. This expression indicates that something surprising (and just a little startling) has occurred.

• **Okay, that does it!** An expression of exasperation is humorous because it shows them that you, the grown-up are out of control or in trouble. Again, as long as they know you're not really serious, this is a good facial cue to let them laugh and respond at the appropriate time. May be accompanied by putting your hands on your hips.

• **Uh-oh.** Yep, you've made a boo-boo, and the kids think it's funny!

• **Awww, how sweet.** This tender look can be tinged with a wee-bit-o-sarcasm or used undiluted, as desired.

• **I'm sorrrry, sooo sorrrry.** An expression to let them know you have done something wrong. It can be used either for comedy effect or to teach a lesson about safety or behavior. Your hands may be clasped in front of you, and your head may be slightly bowed.

• **Good job!** Your look of approval when a magic helper has completed a job—or is in the process of doing a good job—lets all of the children know you are a person they can trust. Giving an expression of approval, both verbal and non-verbal, shows that you are a non-threatening person who likes them.

• **Now, listen up.** Sometimes you have to communicate a serious point. For instance, the show may be over and you want to turn authority back over to a parent or teacher. Your facial expression can let them know that it is time to straighten up and pay serious attention to what you are about to say.

Practice these expressions. Try to communicate the attitude with your face and with your body language. Then find an understanding adult who will watch you make silly faces and try to identify what you are saying.

Are these non-verbal cues really that important? They certainly are. Remember: *Your facial expressions are the punctuation marks of your magic show.* Without them, your act could be a long sentence.

Routines,
Gags,
and
Funny Business
for Children

I created the Jingle Bell Magic *show for pre-schools in 1983. I've presented it every December for day care centers and kindergarten classes. This 11" x 17" poster is printed on a linen-finish paper in three colors—black, red, and green.*

The Imagination Cap
and The Shrinking Glove

Effect

The Imagination Cap is a warm-up routine to help pre-schoolers realize the show will be a fun experience, that the performer is a nice person—and there's nothing to be afraid of. I use this to lead into my routine for the Shrinking Glove.

In the Shrinking Glove routine, the performer removes a pair of gloves he is wearing and gives one to a child. When the magic words are spoken, the child's glove is found to be much smaller than the performer's.

Props Needed

For the Imagination Cap, all you need is your imagination! I got the idea for this bit from Fetaque Sanders, a noted school performer of the 1940s and '50s, who called himself "The Imagination Man." He encouraged children to work with him to create the magic, using their imagination.

The Shrinking Glove is a very small glove which stretches to fit any size hand. It's available in department stores. You'll also need a regular size glove to match the color of the small one. Some magic dealers sell these already packaged. I recommend buying the set from a magic dealer—it's easier than running all over town trying to find matching gloves!

Set-up

Children are usually seated on the floor, awaiting the start of the show. The performer is wearing the magic gloves.

Routine

To appreciate this warm-up, you should first understand my reasons for starting a show in such a simple manner. The typical pre-schooler comes to your show *scared*—or at least, nervous. His father, bless his heart, gets him ready the night before. "Oh, you're going to see the *magician* tomorrow—he'll probably make you disappear!"

Next, the tyke's older brother contributes to the four-year-old's fearful frame of mind. "Yeah, I'll bet he saws you in half before he makes you disappear!"

With this pleasant thought, the tot tumbles into the twilight zone. For all the little guy knows, you *could* make him disappear. And that sawing-in-half trick—how does he know that you, a sane, sensible person, would never do a serious "element of danger trick" for young audiences? All he knows is that two authority figures have told him that you may do mean things to him. And adding to his confusion, they laughed about it!

When he comes to the show the next morning, he has understandable reservations. The performer's job is to ease his mind right away and help him have a good time.

If you begin your act with a bang-flash wand and leap into the middle of the audience yelling, "Howdy, ya little varmits! I'm Chuck the Chuck Wagon Magic Clown!"—you'll have some problems. One kid starts crying. Another one wets his pants. The teachers or parents have to start pulling kids out of the audience like weeds out of an overgrown garden. In the process of uprooting the cry-baby weeds, some perfectly good vegetables (no double meaning intended) get nervous and start crying too.

All in all, this is a very bad way to start a show.

So, what to do? Ease into the performance—make it a friendly visit. I start my pre-school show with an entirely original opening line, which you may feel free to use.

I say, "Hi."

Isn't that a great opener?! It really is, because the children can respond easily. They have no problem saying, "hi" in return.

Then I continue. "My name is Sammy. Sammy Smith, the magician. Today we are going to have the *funniest* magic show you've seen all morning. Does that sound like fun?" Some children admit that it does.

"But to make this magic show work this morning, I'm going to need your help. The first thing you can do to help me is to pick up . . . your imagination cap. Just reach right out in front of you and pick it up." Saying this, I pretend to pick up a cap. I pause while the children pick up *their* imagination caps. Continuing to suit actions to words, I encourage the children to play along and do what I do.

"Now shake it out—hold it up over your head." I have both hands over my head as if to put on a stocking cap.

"Okay, pull it down over your head—but wait! Don't pull it over your ears, because you'll need to *listen* all during the show."

"Now, with your imagination cap on your head, let's pretend." At this point, I drop to my knees to get down on their level.

"Let's pretend that we are sitting on a magic carpet. And we're going to take a trip to a very cold place." Pause and a child will invariably say, "The North Pole!"

By now the children feel more comfortable with you and are going along with your silliness.

"That's a great idea! *The North Pole.* It's probably not crowded this time of year. Let's take off. Everybody ready? Oh! Wait! We haven't fastened our seat belts. Everybody, buckle up!" I reach up and pretend to pull down a shoulder strap and fasten myself in. The children do the same.

"Now let's take off." I hold out my hands as though revving up a motorcycle and make the corresponding *varroom* noise a couple of times. The children, too, will race their engines without being told!

"And we're off!" I stand up and hold my hands in front of me, palms down, and pretend to fly, swinging my hands from side to side.

Now, get this picture—here is the grown-up magic person and a bunch of three- and four-year-olds pretending to fly to the North Pole on a magic carpet! The children are thinking, "This is a crazy magic person! He hasn't even done anything magic—but I like him!" And that is the key: the children have to like you before your magic carpet—or your show—gets off the ground.

"It's nice to be flying on a magic carpet, but it is *cold* up here. Let's all *shiver!*" I wrap my arms around myself and pretend to be cold.

Shielding my eyes and looking below, I say, "Ah, look. There it is—the North Pole! Get ready for a landing! Hold on tight!" We all fly down to land, coming to a screeching halt.

"Here we are at the North Pole. Let's go for a walk along North Pole Boulevard." I march along (standing in place) while the children rock back and forth, pretending to walk.

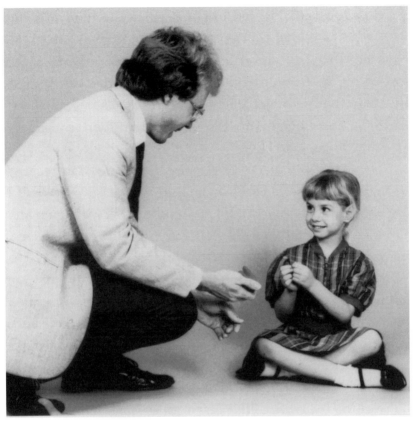

"I'll keep one glove for myself, and I'll give one to you."

I do not let any children stand up. If one starts to rise, I say, "Oh, keep your seat, please, and let's keep pretending."

We march along for a few seconds, then I say, "Hold it! Everybody stop! You won't believe what I just saw! I just saw a little girl here at the North Pole, and she is not wearing any *gloves*." I gesture toward a girl on the front row—I try to spot a brave one. At this point, I do not run over to her, because I don't want her to think that I am going to drag her up front with me. I merely gesture toward her from about six fee away.

I do want the children to get used to the idea of being involved in the show. So I get one girl to help from where she is seated. I say, good-naturedly, "You'll freeze here at the North Pole without any gloves! What's your name?" I am still about five or six feet from her, and I sometimes step back a little as I ask her name. She responds in her shy, giggly little girl voice, "Rebekah."

Now I take the direct pressure off of her by addressing the rest of the audience. "Do you know what I would do if I saw Rebekah at the North Pole, and she wasn't wearing any gloves? Know what I'd do? I would try to give her my gloves. But you know how nice Rebekah is.

"She is so polite that she would probably say, 'Oh, no thank you, I'm fine, thanks.'" I say this is in a high-pitched voice, imitating a little girl. The children think this is very funny. I pause after giving the little girl's reply to let them laugh.

Then I continue. "I would say, 'Now, Rebekah, you know you're going to be too cold. You've got to have some gloves.'"

Now back to the little girl imitation: "Oh, no, really, I'm fine. You keep them, please." I pause and wait for more laughs.

"Well, Rebekah and I would have a little argument about this, but finally, we would agree to share. I would keep one for myself, and Rebekah would take the other one." Saying this, I remove the regular glove so they can see its actual size. I fold it a couple times, then I remove the gimmicked glove, roll it up, and hand it to the girl. She will usually hold on to it. If she refuses, simply drop it on the floor in front of her.

"And then I would say the magic words, 'Hocus Pocus—
Bow-legged Locust!' [Pause.] And we would have one glove
just right for me [I let mine unroll—it's still the same size]
and one just right for Rebekah." I lean down and pick up her
glove, shaking it out to show its size, then hold it next to mine
for comparison.

Then I pause. Sometimes I wait two seconds, sometimes
ten. But always a child will say with glee, "One's big and
one's little!" And then the realization of what has happened
will ripple through the audience. The children will realize
you aren't going to saw them in half, this *is* a funny magic
show, and they are going to have a good time.

The Shrinking Glove.

Balancing a balloon on Seymour's nose. The children will point out that you haven't blown up the balloon.

Seymour the Seal

Effect

A ball, previously vanished, appears on the nose of a wooden seal named Seymour.

Props Needed

This is usually sold as *Sammy the Seal* (which I renamed Seymour since Sammy is *my* name, and I didn't want to be upstaged by a painted piece of pine!) The normal use for this prop is for a previously selected playing card to appear on the nose of the seal. An inflated balloon, tied to his nose, pops and leaves the card in its place. In my routine, I use a balloon, but no playing cards. Instead, a previously vanished sponge ball appears balanced on the Seymour's nose.

Set-up

Clip a two- or three-inch sponge ball to the gimmick and secure the spring-loaded mechanism so the ball is hidden behind the seal. Leave an uninflated balloon on the table.

Routine

When David Ginn saw me perform *Seymour the Seal* a few years ago, he was surprised. Not by the effect, but by the response of the children—they didn't cry when the balloon popped!

As I mentioned earlier, I do not like tricks with popping balloons or other loud noises. But this routine is an exception—and I'll show you why.

Prior to introducing Seymour the Seal, I perform a routine with sponge balls. At the end of the routine, a child is given one of the balls. But he quickly discovers that the ball has vanished. "Do you have the ball?" I ask him. He denies it, so I close out the routine by saying, "Well, John is certainly a tricky boy. Maybe that ball will turn up later on, but for now, let's all clap for John the Magician!" We all applaud, the trick is finished, and we move on to the next routine, *Seymour the Seal*.

To begin with, Seymour the Seal is on my table, covered with a silk handkerchief.

I introduce him: "Ladies and gentlemen, we have a special guest star with us today. His name is Seymour the Seal. Seymour is going to balance a balloon on the end of his nose. Would you like to see that? Well, let me get him to come out here. He has been hiding under this handkerchief. I'll just take it off so he can . . . Seymour [see more]. Let's welcome him to the show with a big round of applause!"

I uncover Seymour as the children clap for him. Then I pick up the balloon. A timid child may be thinking (or, more likely, *feeling*), "Oh, no! He's going to blow up that balloon. It could pop and make a loud noise, and I don't like loud noises!" But they are quickly reassured when they see that I am *not* going to inflate it.

Holding up the balloon, I say, "Seymour is going to balance this balloon on the end of his nose, with no hands . . . or flippers." Then I hold the uninflated balloon high in the air over Seymour, in a semi-dramatic pose. I slowly lower the balloon toward his nose. The children are very attentive during this procedure. Finally, the balloon arrives at the tip of his nose. I release it, step away, and look triumphantly toward the audience. But the balloon quickly falls forward off his nose and lands on the table. The children laugh at this flop. Some of them may say, patronizingly, "You have to blow it up!" And that is a major step toward their future fearlessness about the balloon: they have *told* you to blow it up.

"Oh, I have to blow the balloon up?" I ask. They respond affirmatively. I tilt my head back and hold the balloon a few inches over my face and blow. I am literally blowing the balloon *up*. This is a point of exasperation for the children. They now insist that you blow it up the *right* way!

"Okay, okay" I say, and I take a deep breath to inflate the balloon. Then I stop. I look at them anxiously. "I'm afraid." The children laugh that you, the grown-up, are afraid of a balloon!

"But I'll do it . . . for you." I step back from the audience a few feet to further eliminate any possibility of a fraidy-cat consciousness among the children.

Blowing the balloon up!

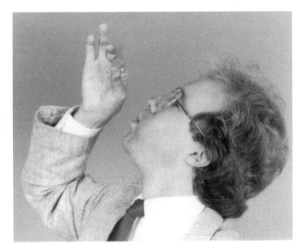

Holding the balloon to my mouth as though I am ready to inflate it, I stretch it a couple of times. After one of the stretches, I take a deep breath and then allow the balloon to snap me in the mouth. The children howl! To make sure *I* don't howl, I really let it snap my fingers, not my lips.

The children settle down, and I try again. I take a deep breath and inflate the balloon a few inches. Then I stop, pinching the balloon to keep it inflated. I start to say something, but my remarks are cut off just at that moment as I accidentally allow the air to escape and blow into my face. The balloon makes a comical sputtering noise and I am flustered by the "unexpected" blast of (hot) air.

Once again, I take a deep breath and inflate the balloon a few inches. Another deep breath, and with great effort the balloon inflates a couple more inches. Then, as if tired of this method, I grip the balloon with one hand and hold it up to my mouth, ready to blow. I fold my other arm into a wing and begin flapping vigorously!

As I flap, the balloon inflates until it is almost completely full. Then I begin to tie it. I look a little apprehensive and comment, "I hope it doesn't pop!" But I successfully tie it off.

Raising the balloon high over the seal's head, I announce, "And now, ladies and gentlemen, the amazing Seymour the Seal will balance the balloon on his nose!" I very slowly lower the balloon toward his nose.

Some of the children will begin to say to each other, "Oooh . . . it's going to pop!" The excitement builds, and in most cases their anxiety about the balloon popping is all in good fun. Remember, they *asked* you to inflate the balloon, and they have been giving you instructions on doing it the right way. Also, you, the grown-up, are a little nervous about the balloon. That seems to defuse its threat to the children. They are thinking, "You silly, it's just a balloon!"

When the balloon reaches the seal's nose—and all the children are waiting in breathless anticipation—I say *"Bang!"* in a good, strong voice. They jump in surprise. Then they laugh, realizing they have scared themselves silly. Depending on whether any children appear to be genuinely nervous, I may actually *shout* the word, "bang!" Then they jump to the ceiling and dangle from the fluorescent lights!

After they have laughed and settled back down, I try again. Holding the balloon high above Seymour's head, I lower it slowly. This time when it reaches his nose, I release my grip and step aside with a victorious air. The balloon will stay on his nose for a few seconds, so the children may briefly think it is really balanced. But it quickly falls off and goes bouncing defiantly away. I run after it and bring it back to the seal.

"Seymour, that's *not* funny! Now, please cooperate. You are supposed to balance this balloon on your nose."

I turn to the audience and say seriously, "Okay, let's try it again." I repeat the action of holding the balloon in the air and lowering it slowly. Once again I release the balloon and of course, Seymour does *not* balance it—to my consternation.

"Well, that does it! If Seymour won't balance the balloon, I'll have to *tie* it onto his nose! The show *must* go on!" Then I fasten the balloon to the ring on the tip of the seal's nose, and this time it stays.

"Well, that is not a great trick, but the balloon *is* on the

The balloon pops, and in its place is a previously vanished ball. It was a better trick than I expected!

end of his nose. So . . . don't give Seymour a *big* round of applause, but let's at least give him a little hand." I lead a light round of applause. While the children are still clapping, I stop and let my hand move to the base, which is supporting the seal. I release the trigger to pop the balloon. It pops suddenly (how else could a balloon pop?) and reveals the sponge ball.

I jump and look surprised, but I don't notice the ball. I let the children point it out, which they will do with great excitement. It dawns on them that this is the missing ball from the previous trick, and they will call out, "Look! It's the ball!"

The balloon has popped and made a loud noise, but it didn't frighten them. They had previously associated the balloon with fun and silliness and when it popped, they were busy clapping. It was all over before they had time to worry!

I pick up the seal and say, "Seymour certainly fooled me. He did a better trick than I was expecting, so let's give him a *big* round of applause after all!"

Some people will do anything to earn a living.

Ernie the Elf

Effect

The performer tells (and demonstrates) the story of Ernie the Elf, who thought his Christmas present from Santa was empty. When he opened the gift on Christmas day, however, it was filled with colorful surprises!

Props Needed

(1) A Square-Circle production box, consisting of two nesting tubes—usually a cylinder within a box—which may be shown empty before producing a large load of streamers, silks, or other items. (Available from most magic dealers.) Mine is actually a "Square-Square," since the inner tube is not cylindrical but rectangular. The Square-Circle represents Ernie the Elf's Christmas gift from Santa Claus.

Square-Circles sometimes come with weird designs painted on them. If yours is not artfully designed (tacky), cover it with Christmas wrapping paper.

(2) A lid for the gift. Cut a piece of cardboard slightly larger than the outside box of the Square-Circle, cover it with wrapping paper, and put a large bow in the center.

(3) A miniature Santa Claus doll or some other cute figure to be used as the final production (available from many greeting card shops).

(4) Twenty-five feet or more of gold or silver Christmas garland.

(5) An instrumental recording of Christmas music. I like electronically recorded music for this purpose. Select a

sentimental tune, such as "The Christmas Song (Chestnuts Roasting On an Open Fire)."

(6) An elf hat.

(7) A long rubber nose, available from magic and novelty stores.

Set-up

Place the Santa Claus doll (or other figure you will use for the final production) in the bottom of the load chamber. Next, wind the garland into a coil and put it into the chamber on top of the doll. My box holds 25 feet, but use as much as yours will contain.

Put the rubber nose in your jacket pocket, and place the elf hat on or behind your table.

In addition to the box-within-a-box that the audience knows about, the gift has a secret third inner box which contains a small Santa Claus doll and 25 feet of gold Christmas garland.

Routine

I've performed this routine in my Christmas show, *Jingle Bell Magic*, since 1983. Young children love to see magic presented in story form. They listen very attentively, and they genuinely care about the outcome of the story.

I begin the routine by saying, "Today, my friend Ernie the Elf was planning to come to the show. But things have been so busy up at the North Pole, getting ready for Christmas, he was not able to get away. So instead, I'm going to show you a story set to music about something that happened to Ernie one Christmas not long ago.

"I brought my six-piece band to play the music for us. [I pick up my tape recorder.] My six-piece band: a tape recorder, a tape, and four batteries! Maestro, some elf music, please!" I press the play button and turn my back toward the audience. The music begins, and the children can see that I am getting dressed for the routine: I put on the elf hat—still facing away from them—and I put on the long nose. They don't see exactly what I'm doing, so when I turn around, the nose gets a big laugh.

As I turn to face them, I say, "This is the story of Ernie the Elf." I pause to let them laugh at the long nose.

Sometimes, for the teachers' benefit, I'll add, "And this goes to show that some people will do anything to earn a living!"

I continue: "A few days before Christmas a few years ago, Ernie was in Santa's workshop cleaning up while the other elves were outside on the playground.

"He was sweeping the shop and doing a good job. And when he was through, like a good elf, he went to the closet to put the broom away. But when Ernie opened the closet door, [taking on a secretive tone of voice] he noticed something high on a shelf—it was a Christmas present!

"Ernie took it down to get a closer look, and guess whose name was on the box! That's right! It said, 'To Ernie, from . . . Santa Claus!' Boy, he was excited! Now you know, he should have waited until Christmas. Ernie knew it, too—but he *didn't* wait. He very carefully removed the ribbon . . . he took off the lid . . . and he looked inside the box. [With excitement] And do you know what he saw? [With a disappointed tone] *Nothing* . . . except another box . . . and his nose. But when you have an elf nose like Ernie's, you can always see that."

As I make these comments, I pick up the outer box, leaving the inner box on the table. I show the outer box empty, spin it around, and look through it toward the audience as I am saying, ". . . and his nose. But when you have an elf nose like Ernie's . . ."

I replace the outer box. "Next he looked inside the other box—and do you know what he saw?" I pull out the inner box and look through it as I say, "Nothing. Except his own . . . nose.

"Ernie was very disappointed." I replace the inner box.

"He put the lid back on his present and tied the ribbon just as he had found it." I pretend to tie a bow, though the bow is actually still on the lid, which I have now replaced.

"Ernie put the present back into the closet, and he went to his room, where he cried for a long, long time." I put my head down into my hands and sob in an over-dramatic, comical manner. Then I stop short and continue the story.

"Finally, Christmas day rolled around, and all of the

Ernie's present from Santa Claus. The appearance of this little Santa Claus doll usually brings on a wave of "ahs" and "awws."

elves were *very* excited. But there was one elf who wasn't very happy, and his name was . . . Ernie. That's right.

"But Ernie was a good sport. He didn't complain at all, and when it was his turn to open his gift, he untied the ribbon and took off the lid and . . ." I say this with a bit of despondency, but as I look down into the top of the gift, my face suddenly brightens.

I look up excitedly and say, "But this time it *wasn't* empty. It was filled with beautiful Christmas garland!" I begin slowly pulling out the garland. I use both hands, exaggerating the motions to make it look like a *very* long stream of garland. Often, the children will ask, "Where did you get all of that!"

As I near the end of the garland, I say, "And just when Ernie thought it would never end . . . [I let the last of the garland slip through my fingers to join the pile on the floor] . . . it did. But Ernie took one last look inside the box . . . and there was his present from Santa Claus, a miniature Santa Claus doll!"

I say the phrase "a miniature Santa Claus doll" with a slow, "aw, how sweet" tone of voice, and as I say "doll," the children will frequently say "awww" in unison! I hold the Santa figure up for display and say, "And Ernie the Elf had a very merry Christmas . . . and a happy New Year!" As the music ends, I remove my elf hat and take a sweeping bow.

*Because you have
occasional low spells
of despondence,
don't despair.
The sun has
a sinking spell
every night but
it rises again
all right the next
morning.*

–Henry Van Dyke

*Unknown to me, Alice the Alligator moves in with jaws wide open!
This is one of several puppet routines I've included in my magic
shows. Puppets add variety—and kids like them. Me, too!*

Alice the Alligator

Effect

No magic here, except for the magic of making children laugh with a simple hand-puppet.

Props Needed

An alligator hand-puppet. I use a cloth puppet, though a wooden Punch and Judy alligator would also work.

Set-up

The puppet is backstage (in your suitcase or behind your table).

Routine

I became interested in using a puppet routine in my shows when I discovered how much children enjoy routines with *characters*. They like magic, of course, but they are strongly attracted to make-believe figures. For instance, you may do a great routine with a rope. But if the rope becomes Sam the Silly Snake, the children will be even more delighted with the trick. So I wondered if I could incorporate a simple puppet routine into my show. The answer was yes, and for the past eight or nine years I have used a puppet in almost every show for pre-school children.

When I want to bring out a personality prop—a puppet, a silk which will become Harry the Happy Handkerchief, etc.—I make a formal introduction to the audience. "Ladies and gentlemen, we have a special guest star with us today, waiting backstage, even as I speak.

"I don't want to scare anyone, but our special guest star today is Alice the Alligator." I turn toward my suitcase, which is propped open and covered with a colorful silk.

"Alice, are you ready?"

Turning back to the children I say, "I am very happy to have Alice as our guest this morning, because she has just written a new book called *Alligatorology* on how to overcome the fear of alligators."

Looking toward the suitcase, I say, "Come on out here, Alice, and tell us about your new book."

I put the puppet on my right hand and bring it into view. "Here she is, ladies and gentlemen, Alice the Alligator. Let's give her a nice round of applause and welcome her to our show." Alice takes a few bows.

I hold the puppet up to my face level about six inches from my right cheek. As I start to speak, I slowly turn the puppet toward my face until its mouth is about an inch away. "As I mentioned, Alice has written a new book. It's called, *Alligatorology*, and I want to say . . ."

I suddenly notice how close the puppet is to my face. I turn to look at the alligator, "Excuse me, Alice. Nothing personal, but if you don't mind, just stand over here. Thanks." I move the puppet away from me a foot or so and turn her face back toward the audience. Then I face the audience again and resume my spiel.

"As I was saying, Alice has written a wonderful book on how *not* to be afraid of alligators." Just then I notice that Alice has turned toward me again and has moved in too close for comfort.

This time, I am a little impatient. "Alice, please! Stand over here while I tell them about your book!" I push her away even farther this time. "Please! Thank you!" I try to regain my composure.

"Ah, yes. As I was saying. I used to be afraid of alligators, but not any more. Not since I read *Alligatorology*. Why, now I could look the toughest, meanest, most ferocious alligator right in the face, and it wouldn't scare me one bit." As I say this, Alice is moving in toward me, this time with her mouth open. When I say the final line, "and it wouldn't scare me one

Alice the Alligator scares her host.

How to put an alligator to sleep. Warning: this only works with puppets!

bit," Alice is next to me with jaws wide open. I suddenly notice her and let out a terrified scream, putting my left hand in front of my face in self-defense, then beating Alice away from me as I have a fit!

"Get back! Get back you alligator, you! Get back!" I slap her on the nose a couple of times before coming to my senses. Suddenly I stop.

"Oh, Alice, I'm sorry! I don't know what came over me! I want to apologize for bonking you on the snout!" But Alice turns toward me with cool indifference. She slowly opens her jaws again and begins moving in my direction.

"Uh, Alice. Wait, now, Alice. Let's be reasonable. I didn't mean to get so upset. I apologize!" With Alice moving toward me, I back up until I'm against the wall, if possible, or as far as I can go so it looks as though I am pinned in.

Then Alice makes her final move. She approaches my face and . . . kisses me with a loud smack, right on the lips! I look totally disgusted; the children laugh hysterically.

"That's disgusting! I could get alligator cooties! Ugh!" Unknown to me, Alice begins rubbing her snout against my jacket, as if to wipe off *my* cooties!

When the children calm down from their hysteria, I say, "Now, seriously, before Alice has to go, I would like to show you how to put an alligator to sleep. The first thing you do is to turn the gator over on its back. [I flip Alice over, slipping the puppet off my hand and letting it rest in my left palm.] Then, you slowly rub the alligator's stomach."

I start to rub Alice's stomach, then I stop and look directly at the audience. "Warning! This only works with puppets! Don't try it with a real alligator! If you ever see a *real* alligator nearby, the best thing to do is—*leave!* Now, back to Alice."

I rub her stomach in a circular motion, saying in a hypnotic voice, "You are getting sleepy. Sleep, sleep, go to sleep." I pause, showing that Alice is absolutely still.

[In a whisper] "Let's say good-bye to Alice the Alligator," then I gently put her away.

Optional Gag

Here is a gag *I* can get away with. You may find it funny, but use caution. It has to be done in a manner that seems completely innocent and free of malice!

After I say, "Sleep, sleep, go to sleep" in a soft tone of voice, I gently move Alice toward the suitcase. Then I suddenly fling [slam?] the puppet down into the suitcase. It hits an empty cardboard box, which makes a very loud *thunk*! I turn, completely unaware that I've just knocked out my special guest star, and immediately go into the next effect.

I have most frequently used this gag when school-age children are mixed with pre-schoolers. This bit of sarcasm appeals to the eight- and nine-year-olds. They usually laugh heartily. I sometimes look back to the suitcase in surprise and remark, "Look at that—she's already sound asleep!"

The Magic of Summer *made its debut in 1982, though this poster didn't come along until 1984. I've presented summertime shows every year since 1982, including such routines as Seymour the Seal, Alice the Alligator, and Rocky the Raccoon.*

Rocky's head gets stuck in his glass after he finishes drinking his milk. Or is he deliberately holding the glass so he can give me a few whacks?

Rocky the Raccoon
(With a Safety Message)

Effect

The performer introduces a realistic raccoon named Rocky. Between the raccoon's antics, the performer works in a safety message about not approaching wild animals.

Props Needed

(1) A spring raccoon, sold in magic and novelty stores.

(2) An opaque plastic cup.

Set-up

Both the raccoon and plastic cup are out of sight until the routine begins. The main preparation necessary is simply practice. Work with the raccoon to make it look realistic. If you have a chance to see David Williamson's routine on video tape or in person, you are in for a treat! His handling is perfect, and the routine is hilarious. It is amazing how much mileage he can get from a spring raccoon in performances for adults. Children react in a similarly delighted manner if you learn to make the raccoon look real.

Routine

"How many of you would like to see my pet raccoon, Rocky? Great! Rocky is waiting backstage right now. [Looking toward my suitcase.] Rocky, come out here. I want you to meet my friends who have been so nice during the show

Rocky the Raccoon has a drink of milk after finishing a snack. Extremely thirsty, he plunges head first into the cup.

today. [Pause.] Rocky. You what? You're putting on your make-up? Well, hurry up!

"While we're waiting on Rocky the Raccoon, let me ask you a question. If you saw Rocky out on the playground, how many of you would pet him? Just raise your hand." Many of the children will raise their hands. Maybe they wouldn't pet just any raccoon, but surely Rocky would be okay!

"Uh-oh! That was a trick question. I certainly hope that *none* of you would pet Rocky if you saw him on the playground. Do you know why? Well, Rocky is a nice raccoon—he wouldn't hurt anybody. But there are a lot of wild animals *who look a lot like Rocky.* They look cute and cuddly, but they may not be safe to pet. Some animals look nice, but they may be sick . . . they could have a disease called rabies, which makes them do mean things they wouldn't normally do . . . like bite!

"So, I hope nobody here will ever even think about touching or getting near an animal you see outside that you don't know.

"But now, let's see if Rocky is ready to come out here. He is a good raccoon. Wouldn't hurt a flea. [Under my breath] That's why he has so many. Rocky! Come on out!" I reach back to pick him up. As I bring him into view, he is wiggling around in my arms, looking out toward the audience.

"Here he is, Rocky the Rockin' Raccoon! Everybody, say *hi* to Rocky." The children are delighted with Rocky. Suddenly he turns his head to the right and stares at a girl on the front row. I notice him staring and say, "Rocky, quit staring at that little girl!" He turns back toward the center of the audience as I apologize to her. "Sorry about that."

"Now, bless his heart, Rocky is probably hungry by this time of the morning. I've got a little Raccoon food here in my pocket. Let's feed him." Holding Rocky in my right arm, I reach into my pocket with my left hand and bring out an imaginary handful of food. The children don't know that it is imaginary since I never let them see into my hand. As I am getting Rocky's snack, he continues to look around at the audience.

Rocky spots the food and swings around to my left hand. He starts eating ravenously for about ten seconds, then he looks up, as if to say, "No more?" I straighten out my hand, showing that it is empty.

"Look at that! Rocky must have been starving! I'll give him a little more." Before I can repeat the process, Rocky has swung his head over to the right again and is staring at the same little girl. I catch him doing that and grab his head, pulling him back over. "Rocky, cut it out! [To the girl.] Sorry about that!"

I bring out some more "food" and Rocky quickly devours it. The children think it is funny that he eats so fast and then looks around for more.

"Sorry, Rocky, but that is all the food I have." He wiggles up to my ear to tell me something.

"You want something to drink? Okay, let me get it for you." While I am not looking, Rocky turns toward the same little girl and stares at her. I catch him, reprimand him, and apologize to the girl again.

"Now I'm going to get a glass of milk for Rocky. That's his favorite." As I bring out the plastic cup, I handle it gingerly, as though not to spill any of the milk. (Of course, the cup is empty, but a little acting can convince the children otherwise.)

"Here you go, Rocky. Have a drink." Rocky sniffs the edge of the cup, then begins drinking. He goes deeper and deeper into the cup until his head is completely inside. However, I do not notice, because I am busy talking to the audience.

"Well, I hope you will always remember what we were talking about . . . not to ever pet strange animals, or even get close to them." By this time, the raccoon's head is completely engulfed by the cup, and Rocky is flailing his head around,

Rocky tries to kiss a girl on the front row. Rocky!

trying to free himself. I continue talking about the importance of being safe with wild animals. Finally, Rocky begins pounding his head (and the cup) against my chest to get my attention. The children laugh.

At last, I notice. Horrified, I say, "Oh, Rocky! I'm sorry! You drank that milk faster than I expected." I pull the cup off of his head and toss it aside. Rocky continues to wiggle around and look at the audience. He scurries up to my ear to tell me something.

"Oh, all right. If you insist. [To the audience.] Rocky wants to tell this little girl a secret." I look toward the girl he has repeatedly stared at during the routine.

"Rocky wants to tell you something." I make sure she does not look frightened. Most of the time, the girl is quite delighted. I walk over to her, holding Rocky. I kneel down beside her. Rocky looks at her and slowly turns to whisper something to her—but he quickly stops and kisses her on the cheek! I make a loud smacking noise at the same time.

"Rocky!" I stand up and carry him away from her. "Rocky, I can't believe you just kissed that girl!" The children, including the victim of Rocky's crush, laugh gleefully.

"We had better put Rocky away before he causes any more trouble. Let's say good-bye now to Rocky the Rockin' Raccoon!"

Cautions

Spring raccoons have become popular items to sell at some theme parks and other tourist locations. One gag that is frequently used by the demonstrator is having the raccoon count to three. The performer holds the raccoon up and slams his head into a post or against a table three times, counting with each blow. "[Whack!] *one*, [whack!] *two*, [whack!] *three!*" I will admit that this is a very funny gag— for adults. But it should not—*absolutely not*—be used with pre-school children.

Why? *Because the children think that Rocky is real.* They would be crushed if they thought that you, their hero, were deliberately hurting an innocent animal. In the *Alice the Alligator* routine, I mentioned the optional gag of throwing the alligator into the suitcase. This is a different situation, because the alligator is obviously a puppet. The raccoon, on the other hand, can even be made to look realistic to adults.

In fact, sometimes during the routine, children will say, "Is he real?" I reply, "Yes. In a former life, yes." The adults present will laugh at the gag. All the children hear is the *yes* reply.

If I am asked again, "Is he real?" I say, "Rocky is the *realest* raccoon I ever had."

They never ask if Alice the Alligator is real.

*Most
of the shadows
of this life
are caused
by standing
in one's own
sunshine.*

–Ralph Waldo Emerson

Maxwell's Blooming Bouquet

Effect

The performer displays a bouquet of yellow flowers. The flowers are plucked off, and unknown to the performer, a new multi-colored set of flowers keeps appearing and disappearing.

Props Needed

A blooming bouquet. The inexpensive model made in India is satisfactory, although versions costing hundreds of dollars are also available.

Set-up

Retract the multi-colored flowers into the bouquet and load the yellow flowers (or whatever color your set comes with). Place the bouquet on your table.

Routine

This routine is based on Trevor Lewis' idea of letting the flowers appear and disappear literally behind your back. (See his *Parade* in the *Linking Ring*, May, 1978. My version of Trevor's routine is included here with his permission.) I added some sound effects, a simple safety message, and included an imaginary character, Maxwell the Monster.

"Today, my friend Maxwell the Monster was going to come to the show with me, but I haven't seen him anywhere. That's too bad, because he was going to show you his favorite

Trevor Lewis, whose clever routine for the Blooming Bouquet inspired my own presentation.

magic trick, the Great Flower Trick. It is his favorite because Maxwell the Monster loves flowers. He loves to smell flowers, but do you know what? He also likes to *eat* them! That's disgusting, isn't it? But he's a *monster*, and we are *people*. We would never, ever put flowers in our mouths, because some flowers could be . . . poisonous, that's right! But when you are a monster, you can get away with a lot of things. I know I did when *I* was a little monster.

"But let me show you how Maxwell would perform the Great Flower Trick. First, he would pick off the flowers one at a time. Like this." I deliberately pluck a flower off, making a popping noise with my mouth as I do so. I look at the flower, then toss it into my suitcase, making a whistling noise as it sails through the air. I follow it with my eyes, and as it lands, make an exploding noise. I repeat this process three more times, until I'm left with one bloom on the bouquet.

I tug on the flower, struggle with it a moment, then finally get it loose. I make a louder, different noise, as though the flower is being torn off the bouquet. I do a double-take at the bloom, then toss it along with the others, following its path through the air until it lands. I look, expectantly, waiting for the explosion. After a five-second delay, I make a louder exploding noise and look back at the audience in surprise.

These noises really make the routine. Pre-schoolers think they are very funny. It keeps their attention and

Flowers appear on the bouquet while I'm looking for the magic wand.

makes them laugh. I know this is silly stuff, but pre-schoolers are silly kids!

I am now holding a bare bouquet—all leaves and no flowers. "Next Maxwell the Monster would hold out his great big monster fingers like this [I hold my right hand in front of me] and wiggle his fingers toward the bouquet. Here—everybody help me. Hold your fingers out. Now wiggle them and say the magic words, 'Hocus Pocus, fish bones choke us!'"

I look at the bouquet. It is not responding. "Hmmm. Maybe I need to get my magic wand." I put the bouquet under my arm—as in Trevor Lewis' routine—then turn around to find my magic wand. As the bouquet goes under my arm, I push the secret lever to make the new flowers appear. The children don't see them until I have my back to them. Then they scream—with delight! Without finding my magic wand, I turn back around to see what they are talking about. As I turn around, I operate the lever to pull the flowers back in.

"The flowers? Yes, we are going to get some flowers on here, but I need to find my magic wand." I remove the bouquet from under my arm, and there are no flowers on it! Another scream.

"Now, just a minute while I find that magic wand." I repeat the move, placing the bouquet under my arm, pushing the lever, and turning around. The children again see the flowers, and they don't keep it a secret.

I turn back around, drawing the flowers back into the bouquet. "The what? The flowers? There are no flowers here." I bring the bouquet out from under my arm and, of

"There are no flowers here!"

course, it has no flowers. The children protest that they *were* there. I cross my arms so the bouquet, in my right hand, is on my left side, out of my line of vision.

"You cannot trick me. There are no flowers . . ." At that point, I push the lever so the flowers reappear. Now I am facing them *and* they see the flowers, so they try harder than ever to get me to look.

"There are no flowers here! You can't trick me!" I uncross my arms and bring the bouquet up to take a look for myself.

*"I refuse to look!
You're just trying to
play a trick on me!"*

As I do, I operate the slide, causing the flowers to vanish. By
the time the bouquet is back in my line of vision, the flowers
are gone.

I hold the bouquet beside my face by my right cheek. "You
are not going to fool me. There have not been any flowers,
there are not now any flowers, and there . . ." At this point,
I cause the flowers to reappear. They are right beside my
face, causing the children to announce the fact with tremendous energy!

To their relief, this time I *do* notice. I jump, startled at the
sudden appearance of flowers! "Look at that! *There are
flowers here!* Why didn't somebody tell me!" When the

audience protests that they *have* been trying to tell me, I say, "Oh. You did tell me? Well I guess I'll have to be a better listener next time. But for now, let's give Maxwell the Monster, wherever he is, a big hand for a great trick!"

Afterthoughts

The response to this routine is so noisy, I find it is best to follow it with a routine that involves the whole audience's calm participation—such as tying an invisible knot or throwing (quietly) a handful of woofle dust. Begin the new routine in a soft-spoken voice and regain complete control over the audience. The purpose of children's magic is to let them have a good time and exercise their imagination—not to see how loud they can scream.

Trying to wear this hat, after all these years . . .

Monster Hat Farewell

Effect

A colored paper hat is too small to fit the performer. As the hat is unfolded to make it bigger, different colored sides are revealed. The hat gets bigger and bigger, finally ending with the performer wearing a large mask of a comical monster face.

Props Needed

The Monster Hat, a commercial product available from magic dealers, developed by Lu Brent and Ali Bongo.

Set-up

Fold the hat to the smallest size, and you're ready to perform.

Routine

This is a good way to close a show for pre-schoolers, because the end of your show means saying good-bye. *Monster Hat Farewell* incorporates the concept of good-byes.

I first read about the Monster Hat about 10 years ago in David Ginn's fine book, *Children Laugh Louder*. He describes a routine in which his uncle, who is in the Navy, sends him a Christmas gift every year—and this gift, a hat, had a note attached: "This will bring out the real you." Taking those two ideas from David, I came up with the following routine for pre-school children.

David Ginn has performed thousands of shows for children at schools and pre-schools. Here he is in 1989 entertaining a little rat.

In my version, I did not want the child to end up being the monster. I would wear the hat instead. Also, I wanted to tie-in the character of Maxwell the Monster, mentioned in the Blooming Bouquet routine. (Also see the Maxwell routine for Soft Soap in *Big Laughs for Little People*.)

"In just a few minutes, we are going to have to say good-bye. That always makes me a little bit sad, because whenever I say good-bye, I think about my uncle . . . who when I

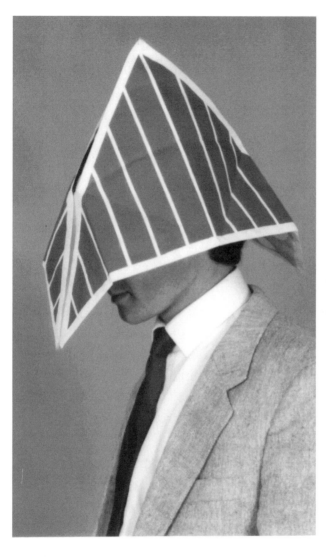

Children laugh when I begin unfolding the hat—especially when I disappear beneath it!

was a little boy, sailed away in a boat to the Far East—Daytona Beach. But before my uncle left, he gave me this hat." (When I mention the boat, I hold the hat upside down and rock it back and forth as though it were a boat bobbing in the water. Then, when I mention *hat*, I turn it over with

the point up so they can see that this could be a hat—
something like a party hat.)

"He said to me, 'Sammy'. . ." I pause and take on a very
tender and nostalgic tone of voice.

"You know, he *always* called me 'Sammy.' You know
why? [Temporarily cheering up.] Because that's my name!"
This gag from Fetaque Sanders has played nicely for older
children, too.

"He said to me, 'Sammy, wear this hat. It will bring out
the real you.' So, I've always liked this hat. I was about four
or five years old when he gave it to me. [I put the little hat
on my head and try to balance it there.] You can see it is a
little bit too small now.

"Nowadays, if I wanted to wear it, I would have to make
it bigger—like this." I open the hat to the next size and place
it on my head in a self-satisfied manner.

"Of course, if my head gets any bigger during the next few
years, I may have to wear this size." I open the hat to the
third largest size. Putting it on my head, the hat covers my
face. The children laugh.

I remove the hat, open the back flap of the remaining
panel and place it on my head. The children laugh louder.

"What has always bothered me, though, is what my uncle
meant when he said this would bring out the real me." I turn
around with my back toward the audience and pull down the
final flap. The monster face is now revealed, but the children
cannot see it yet.

As I turn around, I remark, "I guess I'll never know what
he was talking about." By the time I finish that sentence, I
have turned toward the audience. The children see the

The real me ?

monster face. They immediately laugh and try to tell me about it. Often, they will call out, "It's him—it's the monster!" or "There's Max!"

I remove the hat, ignoring their hyperactivity. Finally, I hear them. "The what? The..." I look at the monster face and scream. "Auhhh! Maxwell! Maxwell the Monster, what are you trying to do? Scare me or something?" The children laugh.

I pretend that Maxwell is trying to tell me something. With my hand beneath the hat, holding it up in puppet-fashion, I bring the monster face near my ear to listen. My eyes open wide. I look completely astonished. With a voice of total amazement I say, "Do you know what Maxwell the Monster just said?" The children lean forward in anticipation.

Then I drop my expression and say in a normal tone of voice, "*Nothing*. He's just a mask!" The teachers laugh.

"But we still don't want to hurt Maxwell's feelings, so let's give him a nice hand for finally showing up!"

Blessed is the man who has found his work.

–Thomas Carlyle

Blessed is the man who has found someone to do his work.

–Elbert Hubbard

"Do you see anything in the bag?"

The Egg, the Bag, and the Magic Hat

Effect

An egg appears and disappears from a small cloth bag. Finally, when the egg cannot be located, the magician checks a magic hat, worn by his audience assistant. The egg is not there—instead, he finds a chicken! Finally, the bag is shown to be completely empty inside and out. The assistant holds the bag, and without the magician's help, causes the egg to reappear!

Props Needed

(1) An Egg Bag and wooden egg, available from magic dealers.

(2) Magic Hat. This is simply a cloth cap with a small secret pocket sewn inside. If you can't find such an item at a magic shop, just sew a small double lining inside the hat near the back. The hat will not be under serious scrutiny.

(3) Terry cloth chicken. Mine was made by Alex Green.

Set-up

Place the chicken into the secret pocket in the hat. Put the egg inside the bag.

Routine

I pick up the Egg Bag and announce that I have something very special inside the bag, and I am going to let one quiet person look and tell everyone what he sees. I select a boy to come up and look. He stands to my right.

"Albert, I would like for you to look into the bag and tell everyone what you see." I hold the bag toward him. The egg is resting in the bottom of the bag, so normally if he looked into the bag, he could see the egg. However, I use both hands to hold open the bag, apparently to let him get a good look. What I am really doing is blocking his view of the egg with my right hand!

I have asked him to tell everyone what he sees. Albert peers into the bag and says, "Nothing." Such an honest lad!

"Ah, I forgot to say the magic words, 'Please' and 'Thank you.'" Without moving the bag, I remove my right hand and snap my fingers. My left hand is still holding the bag in the same position. It is important not to shake the bag or move it around too much. When the egg appears in a moment, it should look as though it has come from nowhere. Holding the bag still makes the appearance seem more amazing.

I continue: "Now, look again." I again use my right hand to open the bag completely. My hand appears to go back to the same position as before, but this time my fingers are out of the way, pressed against the side of the bag, so the boy can see the egg. He usually looks very suprised as he discovers the egg.

"What do you see?" I ask.

"An egg!" he exclaims.

"Reach into the bag and bring it out," I suggest. The other children will laugh in surprise to see that an egg really *has* appeared.

The procedure seems so honest: a volunteer at close range has looked into the bag, the magician has snapped his

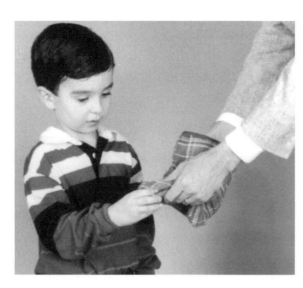

The boy confirms that the egg is in the bag.

or her fingers, and an egg has appeared! I have used this same bluff with older elementary children—and it works!

I take the egg from Albert and hold it up for all to see. "This is a very special egg. It's not just a regular old egg: this is a wooden egg." I rap it on the table three times.

"It was laid by a decoy just a few days ago." Laughs from teachers.

"Now, Albert, I want you to keep your eye on this egg." I move the egg toward him and hold it between his eyes while I shake out the bag. My attention is on the bag, so I fail to see that Albert's eyes are almost crossed trying to watch the egg at such close range.

"Watch close!" I say, as I raise the egg high into the air. "We will now place the egg into the bag." I bring the egg and the bag together, lowering the bag over the egg. I leave my right hand in the bag, holding the egg at my fingertips, while I grasp it from the outside with my left hand. (At this point, I position the egg at the opening of the secret pocket so it will

be an easy matter to slide it completely inside momentarily.)
I wrap the material around the egg so the children can see
the outline and know that the egg really is in the bag.

Next, we check to make sure the egg is there. I sometimes
have the boy feel the egg through the outside of the bag, but
if there is a convenient child on the front row, I step forward,
holding the bag at arm's length (right hand still inside,
holding the egg to the bottom of the bag, and my left hand
still grasping the egg from the outside). "Excuse me, ma'am,
do you feel the egg in the bag?" I let the girl on the front row
check. She affirms that the egg is still there. I do not linger
along the front row, lest other children start calling out to let
them check. One witness is enough.

Stepping back in place and holding the egg and bag high,
I say, "I will now make the egg disappear from the bag—as
quick as a flash, it will completely vanish." So saying, I
pretend to secretly remove the egg with my right hand and
place it under my left arm. I actually leave the egg in the bag,
sliding it all the way into the secret pocket as I remove my
hand.

After I have quickly and suspiciously placed my right
hand under my left arm, I keep my left arm close to my body,
as though hiding the egg. Now, I am still holding the bottom
of the bag with my left hand—pretending to be holding the
egg, though the audience thinks the egg is under my arm—
and the egg is actually in the secret pocket in the Egg Bag,
all the way to the top of the bag.

Continuing my vanishing egg trick, I say with a trium-
phant voice, "On the count of three. One! Two! Three!" Then
I grasp the egg through the bag with my right hand (the

children think I am simply taking hold of the bag, since they are still convinced I've secretly removed the egg) and whisk the bag out of my left hand. I then strike the bag against the heal of my left hand, proving it empty. I ask the boy to reach into the bag, feel all around the bag, and see if he finds the egg. (He, of course, finds nothing.) Meantime, the children begin to announce their suspicions.

"It's under your arm!" they say.

"All right," I concede, "if you think you know where the egg is, raise your hand." At this, I raise my left hand high into the air, inadvertantly showing that the egg is not there. This old gag always gets a big laugh from the adults. I strike the supposedly empty bag against the heal of my left hand again, turn the bag inside out, and say to the boy, "Albert, do you see anything in the bag at all." I hold the bag right up to

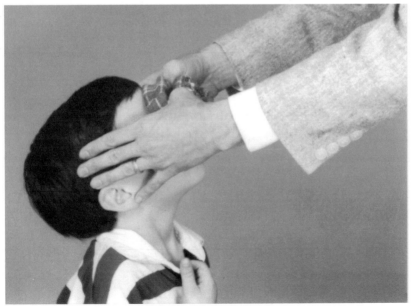

"Do you see anything in the bag now?"

his eyes, completely obstructing his vision. Another laugh.

The child says that he sees nothing at all. "That's because the egg is now under Albert's arm." I take hold of the boy's left arm, pump it up and down a few times while I make a noise like a squawking chicken. Then I hold the bag under his arm and allow the egg to slide secretly out of the pocket back to the bottom of the bag.

I make a few squawking noises and the egg appears from under the boy's arm.

I thoughtlessly drop the Egg Bag on the boy's head as I turn around to get the magic hat.

"Now, Albert, reach into the bag and show us what you find." The boy reaches in and pulls out the egg, to his amazement. The audience usually applauds.

"Let's give Albert another chance to try this trick. This time, I'm going to let him wear a magic hat." I hand the egg to the boy as I drop the bag on top of his head and then turn around to my case. The kids laugh at the bag on top of the boy's head, but I ignore them as I reach into my case and remove the multi-colored hat, which is secretly loaded with the terry cloth chicken.

I turn back around to the boy, but I don't see him. I look around for a moment, then call him. Suddenly, I realize he is under the bag! "Albert! I'm sorry! I thought you were a rug!" I whisk the bag off of his head and replace it with the hat.

"I thought you were a rug!"

The hat looks reminiscent of the uniform of a fast-food restaurant, so I look at him and remark, "Albert, I'll have a Whopper, Jr. with cheese, [pause for laughter], a medium Coke [pause again], and one egg." I take the egg from him and hold it up high.

"We'll place the egg back inside the bag, all the way to the bottom." I repeat the procedure from the first portion of the trick, loading the egg into the secret pocket, and pretend to remove it from the bag. This time, however, I pretend to place the egg under my knee. I bend my leg back, standing on one foot, and hop around a little.

"I will now cause the egg to disappear," I proclaim. The children laugh at your obvious ploy—they *know* it's under your leg!

When I finally hear them, I say, "Pardon? The egg? No, it's just my leg!" And I straighten out my leg, putting both feet on the floor, to show that I *wasn't* holding the egg behind my knee.

"The egg is back under Albert's arm." I repeat the pumping of the boy's arm, accompanied by squawking. This time, though, when he reaches into the bag, he doesn't find anything. I turn the bag inside out as we frantically look for the egg.

Often, a child in the audience will say, "It's in his hat." If not, I look at the hat on the boy's head and comment uncertainly, "Do you . . . do you think . . . the egg could have landed inside that magic hat?" Then, acting as though I'm certain I've found the egg, I triumphantly remove the hat and say, "Albert, reach into the hat and pull it out!" I hold the hat open for him to reach inside. I am actually holding open the secret pocket in the hat so he (but not the audience) can see the terry cloth chicken. Being a wadded up piece of cloth at this point, he won't usually be able to determine what it is. But without further coaxing, the boy usually reaches right in, pulls it out, and holds it up for display.

The boy and the audience break out into hysterics. I don't notice what they're laughing about. "Yes, ladies and gentlemen, the egg has disappeared from the bag, flown through the air, and landed inside Albert's magic hat." Then, for the first time, I see the boy holding up the chicken—he's usually

The egg is not in the hat!

*"That"s not
even a hen!"*

holding it by the head with two fingers while the body sways
back and forth in a ridiculous and amusing manner.

"What? That's not an egg! That's not even a hen!" I snatch
the chicken up and take a closer look.

"We are going to have to put this chicken away." I hold it
up at my eye level, my left hand holding its body, my right
fingertips holding the top of its head.

"Look into my eyes. You are getting sleepy. Very sleepy."
Then I drop the head and allow the chicken to fall limp into
my left hand. This is good for a nice laugh.

"Just relax . . ."

"That's right. You go to sleep." As I turn to put the chicken in my bag, I give its neck a quick wring, adding, "Sleep tight." This quick bit is picked up by the adults, yet I've never had a child say, "You hurt the chicken." They don't understand the significance of wringing a chicken's neck, and this is over in a second anyway. I toss the chicken into my case.

"Albert, we've got to find that egg. Let's make absolutely certain that there's nothing in the bag. Do you see anything in here, anything at all? Reach your hand inside the bag. Do you feel anything? Put your other hand in the bag. Do you find anything in the bag now? Jump inside the bag . . . no,

"Eggscuse me . . ."

just kidding." I turn the bag inside out, then back to inside in, proving it is completely empty. All the while, of course, the egg is concealed in the pocket near the top of the bag, guarded with my right hand.

"You've got to help me, Albert. Hold on to the bag for me while I look for the egg." I give him the bag, in the process allowing the egg to fall silently back into the bottom of the bag. I make sure the boy holds the bag by the top.

Now, two conclusions are possible. The one I prefer is to have the boy look inside the bag and discover the egg on his own while I am looking the other way in search of the egg. When this happens, some very funny reactions are possible. The boy is truly amazed to find the egg. Sometimes, he will remove it from the bag and try desperately to tell me that he's found it. Meantime, I'm looking all over the stage.

The second ending happens when you have such a well-behaved boy that he won't look into the bag without your permission. If I see that the boy is not going to make his own discovery, I search for a few moments, then say to the audience, "I need everyone to help. Hold your hands out in front of you, wiggle your fingers, and say the magic words, "Hocus pocus, bow-legged locust!" After they comply, I ask the boy to reach inside the bag and see if the magic worked. Then he reaches in and pulls out the egg to the excitement and delight of the audience.

"Fantastic, Albert! You and your friends have made the magic work. [To the audience] Let's give Albert a great big round of applause!" I remove the hat from his head and reclaim the egg and bag as I send him back to his seat.

Printed in black and orange on a white enameled paper, this 1985 poster measured 11" x 17". My friend Fetaque Sanders pointed out that the artist should have shaded in one of the children's faces to represent a black or other minority child.

It's the farm, but there are no farm animals. No satellite dish, either!

So, we look for the farm animals, hoping to find the old farm cat. (As I remove each card, I use it to point toward the next picture. This casually shows the back of each card.)

Farmyard Frolics

Effect

A magic cat is found among five picture cards of farm animals. The cat disappears and supposedly has landed on the farm. But on checking the farm (actually a folder with a colorful picture of a farm)—no cat. Then, unseen by the magician, the sly cat begins peeping out from behind the folder to the roaring amusement of the children.

Props Needed

This trick was originally sold by Supreme Magic of England. Some magic shops still carry it. It consists of six 8" x 10" cards: four of them picturing different animals one might find on a farm; another card with a picture of a cat on one side and a duplicate picture of a cow on the other side; and a card with a large question mark.

A flexible straw mat is used to cover the cat card before he disappears.

The next part of the trick is a folder with a picture of a fenced farm on the outside. Inside the folder is a quaint farm house and pastures—but no farm animals.

Finally, on the back of the folder, unseen by the audience, is a cut-out of a cat just like the one on the card. It fits into a shallow pocket on the back of the folder. When the time comes for the cat to reappear, the cut-out cat can be slid out with your thumbs, causing it to peek around the folder.

Supreme sold the trick with two simple stands to hold the folder and the animal cards upright for display.

Set-up

The animals are arranged from front to back as follows: cow, lamb, dog, pig, cat (with the duplicate cow on the reverse side), and the question mark card. The cut-out cat is hidden in the pocket behind the folder.

Routine

"When I was a little boy, I loved to go to the library. In fact, the library is still one of my favorite places to visit.

"When I was little, our librarian was so nice that she would meet me out in front of the library—she wouldn't even make me go inside to get a book! Wasn't that nice of her? One day she met me out front just as I was getting ready to go inside. She said to me, 'Sammy.' And you know, she always called me *Sammy*. You know why? 'Cause that's my name! [The same gag I learned from Fetaque Sanders which I use in the Monster Hat routine. Of course, I don't use this gag twice in the same show.]

"Anyway, she said to me, 'Sammy, here's a book you might enjoy.' [I pick up the folder with the word farm on the outside.] And she handed me a book about a farm. But when I opened the book, there was a beautiful farm house, there were pictures of pastures, but there was something missing . . ." The children will usually say, "No farm animals!"

"That's right," I reply, ". . . and no satellite dish!"

I continue, "But the thing I was most disappointed about was: there was no farm cat. On my grandfather's farm, he always had an old farm cat named Jake. But here in this book—no cat.

"Now, today I brought along some pictures of farm animals, and maybe if we look through them, we can find Jake the cat. Would you like to do that? If we find him, maybe he will do a trick for you, because Jake is a magic cat." I close the folder and set it down before picking up the stack of animal cards.

"The first animal we find is . . . *not* a cat." I turn around the stack of cards so the children can see the first card, the cow. They will call out that it's a cow.

"Well, we'll keep looking. We'll find that cat one way or udder." I take off the cow card and place it behind the others, first using the corner of the cow card to point to the next card

"We'll find that cat one way or udder."

in the stack. That casually shows the back of the cow card, which is simply a printed design.

"The next animal is a . . . that's right, a lamb. That certainly is not a cat." I remove the card with my right hand.

"Then we have a . . . dog." I point to the dog with the upper right corner of the lamb card (from my perspective) before placing the lamb card to the back of the stack.

"This is probably the sheep dog." I begin to remove the dog card.

"The funniest animal on the farm is the . . . [I let them fill in the blank as I finish removing the dog card] . . . *pig*, that's right! This pig walked up to me the other day and said, 'I'm so hot, I'm nearly bakin' [bacon]!' [Pause and wait for laughs.] I guess he never saw such [sausage] heat!" Groans and laughs.

"The next animal we find is . . . " I remove the pig card to reveal the cat card.

The kids enthusiastically shout, "It's the cat! It's Jake the cat!"

I immediately join their excitement, put the pig card behind the stack and say, "Great! Here he is, Jake the magic cat! Are you ready to see him do a magic trick? Okay!"

I begin to pick up the cat card, actually picking up the cat (which has a cow on the back) *and* the secret question mark card (which has a regular card design on the back). With those two cards aside, the children can see that the cow is again at the front of the stack. But they think I've only picked up one card—the cat.

"Keep your eye on ol' Jake the cat. We're going to turn him over for a moment, cover him with a mat, and see if he will disappear!" Saying this, I turn both cards over on the stack.

I briefly slide the question mark card (now in front with its back toward the audience) away from the stack. This action allows a glimpse of the cow—*but this time, it's the cow on the back of the cat card.* The audience thinks they are still seeing the original cow, and they think the card you're holding is the cat. They don't even realize that a question mark card exists.

I put the stack of cards away in my prop case, still holding the question mark card in my right, with the back of the card facing the audience. I speak to the card as though it's still the cat. "Jake, are you ready? Okay!"

I cover the card with the mat and place it on the display stand. "When I snap my fingers, Jake the cat will disappear from the mat, fly invisibly through the air, and land on the farm." I snap my fingers and make a whistling noise as I pretend to follow Jake's path out of the mat, into the air, and into the folder. When Jake supposedly lands in the farm folder, I make an explosion noise, as though Jake has landed very *hard.*

"Now, let's see if he made it." I peek in the top of the folder and say confidently, "Yes! There he is! Now, watch him fly back to the mat!" The children protest—they didn't get to see!

"Do you think that I . . . well, I certainly would not try to trick you! Here—I'll show you, Jake the cat has completely disappeared from the mat." I pick up the mat, secretly holding the cat card behind it.

"There is no cat in this mat!" I pull the bottom of the mat up with my left hand, clipping it between a couple fingers in

While showing the mat empty, I make it obvious that I am trying to conceal a card.

my right hand, meantime allowing the top of the mat to slide down. By flipping the mat over this way a few times, I pretend to be showing that the mat is empty. It's fairly obvious that I am still hiding the card behind the mat: I want the children to point this out.

"Pardon me?" I say, raising my right hand—still holding the card—to my ear. I quickly realize that I have exposed the card. I act embarrasssed as the children tell me that the cat has not disappeared.

"Oh, there's no cat back here," I claim. "The cat has vanished." I now want them to ask me to turn the card around. Of course, the quickest way to get them to ask is to begin putting the card away. As soon as I make a move toward my prop case as though I'm going to dispense with the card, they will protest loudly. They want me to turn it around!

I do the old gag of turning the card around steering-wheel fashion. They protest, "No! The other way!" Then I turn it counter-clockwise. More protests.

"Flip it over? I don't want to make the poor cat dizzy." So saying, I nevertheless flip the card over to reveal that the cat is gone and there remains only a question mark. A wave of gasps and shouts runs through the audience. I, too, am baffled.

"Pardon me? Oops!"

*Jake the magic cat
really has
disappeared!*

"Do you think? . . . could it be? . . . did Jake? . . . do you think he landed in the . . . farmhouse?!" The children, of course, want the folder opened so they can see if the cat is there.

I pick up the folder triumphantly and announce, "And here he is, ladies and gentlemen, it's Jake the magic cat! Let's hear a nice round of applause for Jake . . ." I have now opened the folder and the children can see that Jake is not there. I look down at the picture of the farm in surprise.

"Jake! That's not funny! [To the audience] He was here just a moment ago." I close the folder, still holding it in front of me as I look to the side, calling for Jake. Meantime, using my thumb, I slip the cut-out cat out of the pocket on the back of the folder. I slide it over far enough so he appears to be peeking over the side of the folder. The children go absolutely berserk. There is unbelievable screaming and calling out to let me, the oblivious magician, know that Jake is back!

I turn back to the folder, but of course, Jake slips out of sight and I don't see him. Looking to the other side of the room, still searching for Jake the magic cat, I use my other thumb to slide Jake to the other side so he can peek out at

Jake appears when I'm not looking.

the audience. More screams and laughter. I do this a couple of times, but I try not to let the children get out of hand. Six or seven repetitions of this hide-and-seek would be too much. Three or four times is plenty.

Finally, I look at the audience, still unable to find the cat. I start to speak, and the cat rises up over the top of the folder and snuggles in under my chin. The audience lets me know what has happened. I look down, now pinning the cat to my collar bone as I withdraw the folder. "Jake! Here you are! [To the audience] Well, he did make it after all—not a bad trick for a cardboard cat. Let's give him a nice big hand!"

Jake the magic cat finally makes his reappearance.

Fetaque Sanders was a great entertainer of children—the leading black magician from the 1930s through the 1950s. We spent many hours on his front porch in Nashville, Tennessee discussing magic and comedy. I took this picture in 1989. Even 30 years after his retirement, Fetaque always wore a coat and tie and usually had a hat.

*Whoso
would be
a man
must be a
nonconformist.*

–Ralph Waldo Emerson

The Magic Candy Box

Effect

A dollar bill is placed in a small, empty candy box, rubber-banded for security. The box is given to a child. When the magic words are spoken, the magician opens the box and the money is gone!

Then, in an effort to either regain the money or create something good to eat (candy?) the box is re-rubber-banded and given back to the child. More magic words. On re-opening the box, a six-foot spring snake emerges with the dollar bill trailing behind!

Props Needed

(1) A six-foot spring snake, preferably covered with thin cloth for the smallest possible compression.

(2) Two identical candy boxes. I use the small Valentine's boxes in the shape of a heart.

(3) Two one-dollar bills.

(4) Four heavy rubber bands.

(5) Giant toothbrush.

Set-up

First, you'll need to reinforce the candy boxes. Cut out two pieces of corrugated cardboard the size and shape of each box and glue one to the bottom of each box. Then reinforce the lids of each box by running a thin line of glue around the joint where the top meets the sides of the lid. The boxes need

Trace the outline of the candy boxes onto a piece of currugated cardboard. Then cut out the shapes, get a bottle of glue, and . . .

to be reinforced because one of them will be holding the spring snake, which puts a lot of pressure on typically flimsy candy boxes.

Next staple a dollar bill to the end of the spring snake. Then fold the bill in thirds (zig-zagged) and compress the snake. Place it into one of the candy boxes, securing the lid with two of the thick rubber bands. The boxes I use are small enough to wrap the rubber bands around twice. The pressure of the spring snake may make it necessary to double-wrap the rubber bands anyway. Put this loaded box behind your table or in your prop case, along with the giant toothbrush.

The other candy box rests on your table in view, with the other dollar bill inside and two more rubber bands beside it. During the entire routine, of course, the audience should be unaware of the duplicate box and dollar bill.

Routine

I invite a boy up front to assist me, then begin my patter.

"When I was a little boy, my grandmother sent me a Valentine's Day gift. When I opened the package, inside I found a candy box. [I pick up the box from the table.] But even though it *was* a candy box, do you know what it *wasn't?* A box of candy."

I pause and begin to speak in a secretive, excited tone of voice. "When I opened the box and looked inside, I found..."

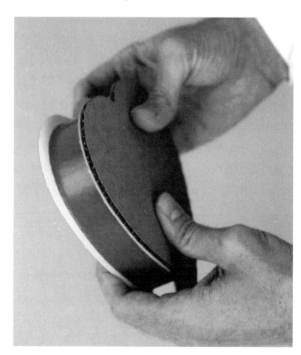

... glue the cardboard to the bottom of each box, to reinforce them.

Staple a dollar bill to the end of the spring snake.

I remove the lid slowly and pause to let the children fill in the blank and say, "Money!" or "A dollar!"

"That's right! A brand-new one-dollar bill! And I've saved this dollar all these years. Since this was a gift from someone special, I have always wondered if this might be magic money—*that maybe if I knew the right magic words,* I could change this into . . . candy or something good to eat. [Pause.] *But I'm sure you don't want me to waste time trying to do that,* so I'll just put this away and get on with the show." The children, of course, will protest. They want to try the trick with the dollar. But amid their pleas, I replace the dollar in the box and start to put on the lid. As I do so, I take it to my prop case, lowering it out of sight. As soon as the box is out of view, I dump the dollar. No fancy sleights—I just turn the box over and let the dollar fall out. I'm still holding the lid with my right hand and the box with my left, just about to put on the lid.

As soon as the dollar falls out (unknown to the audience), I hear what the children have been saying. "Wait a minute. Did you say you *do* want to see if this is a magic dollar?" Then I immediately bring the box back into view. *It has only been out of sight for a moment,* just long enough for me to dispose of the dollar.

"Well, okay . . . if you insist, we'll give it a try."

I turn to the boy. "Wesley, let's wrap this box up with a couple of rubber bands, for security." I pick up the rubber bands.

"But first, let's make sure the dollar is in the box. Look in there and nod your head *yes*." I hold the box to his eyes, barely opening the lid enough for him to peek in. He really can't see anything, but for some reason, he usually nods his head. Why? In the child's mind, you have given an order: look in the box, then nod your head. So, most kids do just as you have said—if you give the order in a direct, confident way. To the other kids, it looks as though the boy is looking for the dollar, then nodding his head *yes* that he sees it. If the child doesn't immediately nod his head, I say, "Nod your head." And he usually nods. This is called magic by bluffing! (It's true that a 12-year-old may be inclined to say, "No, I can't see anything," but in this routine, we are dealing with younger, more easily influenced children!)

After the nod, I finish putting on the lid and then begin to wrap a rubber band around the box. "To make sure nobody can get into the box, we'll put this rubber band around it. And we'll put on this other one to be extra-safe."

To the boy: "Now, Wesley, I'm going to let you hold the box while we say the magic words." I hand the boy the box, getting him to hold it against his stomach so he isn't tempted to shake it. (It's possible that an ambitious kid could shake the box and say, "Hey, I don't hear the money." This has never happened, but why take the chance?

To the audience: "Hold your hands out and wiggle your fingers, and let's say the magic words, 'Hocus-pocus, bow-legged locust!'" Turning to the boy, I ask if he felt anything happen.

"Well, let's see if something magical happened to the money. Maybe there's *more* money—or maybe there's something good to eat!" I take the box from the boy and remove the rubber bands with enthusiasm. Slowly and with an expression of expectation, I lift off the lid.

"And here it is, ladies and gentlemen, the dollar has . . ." I finish removing the lid so the children can see inside. They complete my sentence, "Disappeared!"

With a look of astonishment I examine the box inside and out to find that the money *has* vanished. I look at the box, at the audience, at the boy in utter confusion. "Did you—?" The boy will say that he didn't take the money.

"Well, now, something has backfired. Let's try this again. Maybe we can get the trick to work or at least get the dollar back." I replace the lid and wrap the rubber bands around the box, this time, wrapping each band around twice.

"We'll wrap these around twice to make sure Wesley doesn't pull any more tricks on us!" Then I start to hand the box to the boy.

"Hold it, Wesley. If this trick works, if we do get some candy, you'll need to be prepared. I have just what you need." I turn back to my prop case with the candy box in my left hand. I pick up a giant toothbrush with my right hand and simultaneously drop the empty candy box and pick up the one loaded with the snake. This takes just a second before I come back into view holding the giant toothbrush up in my right hand. The audience does not realize the box has been switched.

"Wesley, if we do get some candy, you'll want to have a toothbrush handy. Did you brush today?" Regardless of the boy's answer, I give his hair a quick swipe with the giant toothbrush. The children laugh.

"Okay. Hold the toothbrush with this hand [putting it in the boy's right hand] and hold on to the candy box with your left hand. Hold it against your stomach just like before." It's especially important that the boy hold the box against his body. Otherwise, he may begin to weigh the box in his hand and note that it's now much heavier.

"Now, everyone help. Reach into the air for a handful of woofle dust. Toss the woofle dust toward the box, and let's say some new magic words: *please* and *thank you*." The children all toss the imaginary dust and say the words.

"Wesley, take the toothbrush and give the box a tap." The boy taps the box, then I take the toothbrush from him and toss it aside. I also take the candy box from him and hold it up, ready to remove the rubber bands.

"And now, ladies and gentlemen, once again . . . let's see if the magic worked." I very deliberately remove the rubber bands, holding the box tightly with my hands to keep it from springing apart too soon. Now, with the box in my hands, I remove the cover and allow the spring snake to jump suddenly into view. I manage to bite the snake and hold it between my teeth as I wrestle with it. Meantime, I toss the box into my prop case to devote my energy to wrestling the snake. The children, of course, will scream and then notice that the dollar is hanging onto the tail of the snake. After they point this out, I look down and discover that they are right.

I hold the tail of the snake up so the dollar is in view and say to the boy, "Wesley, look! We got the dollar back!

"Thank goodness, we had Wesley to help us. The bad news is that there is no candy, but the good news is, tomorrow for snack, everyone gets peanut and snake sandwiches! [Laughter and squeals from the children.] Let's give our fantastic helper, Wesley, a big round of applause." I pat the boy on the back, tell him he was a great helper, then direct him back to his seat.

More Candy Box Thoughts

If you are uncomfortable ditching the dollar in the brazen way I describe, you could make up a gimmicked candy box. Get a piece of white, painted aluminum (or a thin piece of cardboard heavily spray-painted to give it extra weight), cut out to fit in the lid. Then you could place the dollar, folded in half or in thirds, in the bottom of the box. When you put the lid on the box, the flap will fall out of the lid into the box, concealing the dollar. Of course, the flap should be the same color as the interior of the box.

Other thoughts: The smaller the candy box, the better, since it will look all the more amazing to have the six-foot spring snake pop out of a little box. The box I use is just big enough to accommodate the snake.

Credits: David Ginn's *Snake Can Routine* inspired my Magic Candy Box. The red silk David uses is good for stage, but since I present this routine for smaller groups, the dollar is plenty visible and fits into the storyline better. Even if you use David's *Snake Can Routine* for older audiences and larger groups, using a candy box or other container may be better than the now-familiar peanut brittle can. Some children may see the peanut brittle can and *know* there's a snake inside!

The
reward
of a good
deed is
to have
done it.

–Elbert Hubbard

Puff the Magic Rabbit

A cute exchange between the magician and a rabbit-in-the-hat puppet. This is my own version of a very old routine. How old is it? Dick Williams, star of the *Magicland* television show (which ran for 23 years!), says he first saw this routine in the 1940s! (Later, he developed his own very funny routine which is included in his book about television magic, called *Lights! Cameras! Magic!*) But here's my own version which I've used for both children and adults.

Props Needed

(1) Top hat with a rabbit puppet inside. A hole is cut in the back of the hat so the puppet can be operated in semi-concealment.

(2) One piece of rope.

(3) Two brightly colored socks, one bright red, the other bright yellow. You can vary the colors, if you like, but they should be solids.

(The sock gag is the last routine I discussed with Fetaque Sanders, my good friend and show advisor.)

Set-up

Rabbit and hat are in my show case to my left. The rope is in the hat under the rabbit. Also in the case, readily accessible, are the two flashy socks.

Routine

"Ladies and gentlemen, it's time now to bring out our special guest star, Puff the Magic Rabbit. [Looking toward the case.] Puff. Puff. Are you ready? You're what? You're putting on your make-up?" Laughter from kids.

Looking toward the audience: "I have to tell you that Puff is a little bit shy because he's just a puppet, and being a puppet, he doesn't like to go places by himself! But maybe it would help his feelings if you encouraged him to come out by giving him a big round of applause. So here he is, ladies and gentlemen, let's hear it for Puff the Magic Rabbit!" I look expectantly toward the hat as I lead the applause. When he doesn't make an appearance, I look disappointed.

"Look here, Puff, come on out now. We're waiting for you. [Nothing happens.] Oh, I know what the problem is: he's probably mad. He's mad at me because I'm not wearing the birthday present he gave me this year. Puff gave me a pair of socks, and I refuse to wear them. I'll show you why."

I reach into my case and pull out the yellow sock, holding it in front of me for display. "Here it is. [Pause and wait for comments.] I'll show you the other one." I reach into my case and bring out the red sock, holding it up beside the yellow one for comparison. Some child usually says, "They don't match!" or "One's red and one's yellow!"

I reply, "I know they don't *look* like they match, but they *must* match. You know why? [Pause.] 'Cause I've got another pair at home just like 'em!" I pause and wait for the adults to laugh.

The children sometimes laugh. If they don't, I say, "Well, let's see if I can get this rabbit to come out here and explain that joke." More laughter from adults. I toss the socks back into my case.

Addressing the rabbit again, I say, "Puff, now please, come out . . . hey! Stop that! Stop putting on my socks!" I put my hands on my hips and let the children laugh at the thought of Puff putting on my socks.

"Puff, take those socks off your ears!" This gets a nice laugh because the picture of Puff putting on the socks suddenly takes on new meaning. When the laughter dies down, I decide to go in after the rabbit.

"All right. That does it. I'm going to bring him out with my bare hands!" I step behind my case and stoop down completely out of sight. I make some struggling noises and say, "Hey! Stop that! Puff, would you . . ." Then I fling one of the socks high into the air so it flies out of the case, looking as though the rabbit has thrown it out. After laughter, I toss out the other one. In shows where I've previously done a routine with a cloth chicken (*The Egg, the Bag, and the Magic Hat*), I cry out with alarm, "No! Puff! Not that!" Then I fling the chicken into the air. That gets more laughs.

Still speaking from behind my prop case. "All right, everyone. Don't worry. I've got him. Oops! Come on now, Puff, get out of there! [To audience.] He jumped into my hat!" Then I come out with the hat in my left hand and my right hand through the hole in the back and inside the rabbit puppet. The rabbit is still inside the hat, out of sight.

"Okay, Puff, come up and see these nice people." Puff slowly peeks out of the hat and waves a paw. The children will wave back and call out to him.

Now, here's an interesting phenomenon: I've previously told the audience that Puff is a puppet and "he doesn't like to go places by himself." But occasionally at this point, a smart child will call out, "Your hand's inside!"

I reply, "Well, sorry to say, that *is* the way a puppet

works! Now . . ." Then I pause briefly as though taking a breath for the next sentence (actually pausing to allow a few seconds for the line to sink in). Interestingly, that line often will get a strong laugh from the adults. I think it works because it appears to be an ad lib: they don't realize how often a child calls out, "You've got your hand in there!"

Continuing the routine. "Puff the Magic Rabbit is the world's only reading rabbit. He goes to the library every week to check out books. This week he checked out a book about the Great Houdini, a famous magician and escape artist who could get out of anything. So today Puff is going to show you a wonderful magic trick. Probably the best magic trick you've seen in a long time." As I say that Puff will be showing them a trick, Puff shakes his head *no*, unknown to me. The children laugh and point out that he is saying *no*.

Turning to Puff: "What did you say? [Puff whispers in my ear.] You're not going to show them a magic trick? [Puff shakes his head *no*.] Why not? [Puff whispers in my ear.] You don't feel like it? [Shakes his head *no*, then whispers again.] *You are rabbit with an attitude?!* [Howls from children, particularly from older kids in mixed-age audiences.] How would you like to be *rabbit-sawed-in-half?!* [Whispers in my ear.] No need to split hares?" Puff shakes his head *no*.

Now, I address the audience. "Puff says he *will* perform the amazing Houdini Rope Escape out of a hat. A death-defying feat of courage and skill!" Puff begins bowing repeatedly, with obvious pride.

Seeing Puff bowing vigorously, I reprimand him. "Would you cut that out?!" Puff stops.

"Ladies and gentlemen, this is a big moment on the

Puff the Magic Rabbit puppet performing the rope escape out of a hat.

American stage. Let's have a drum roll for Puff the Rabbit. Pat your hands on your knees." The children begin the drum roll, and I take on a circus ringmaster tone of voice. "Yes, ladies and gentlemen, it's the amazing Puff the Magic Rabbit, performing the incredible Houdini Rope Escape out of a hat. It's astounding, it's . . ." While I'm building up the stunt, Puff dives into the hat and grasps the rope between his paws. He pulls it out of the hat into view, pausing long enough for the audience to laugh. Then he flings the rope to the floor. The audience laughs again. Puff bends down over the edge of the hat to look at the rope on the floor. He waves good-bye to the rope with one paw. This gets a big laugh from the adults *and* kids. Next he straightens up and begins bowing.

Meantime, I hear the roar of the audience and look at Puff, who is bowing to all parts of the audience. Looking at him in amazement and semi-disgust, I ask, "What are you doing?"

Puff whispers in my ear. I repeat his comment in disbelief: "The rope escaped from the hat?" Puff again looks toward the floor and waves farewell to the rope. That is just too much for me!

"I can't believe it. I can't believe he did such a ridiculous trick for you. That has got to be the worst magic trick I have ever seen." While I am lambasting Puff, his head droops, unseen by me, and finally he covers his eyes with his paws, puts his head on the brim of the hat, and cries silently. This often evokes great sympathy for the rabbit.

I spot him crying. "Oh, would you look at that. I've hurt his feelings. Come on, Puff, don't be like that. I didn't mean to hurt your feelings. Let's be friends. What do you say?" After a brief pause, Puff lifts his head from the hat, looks at me, and growls fiercely. The audience roars and I jump back. Puff returns to his pouting and crying position.

"Now, please, Puff. Don't be hurt. I didn't mean that I don't like you. I do like you. I just didn't like the trick. But I think you are . . . wonderful. In fact, I think you're the most wonderful, beautiful rabbit in the world." Puff slowly lifts his head and looks at me in amazement. Then he leans straight into my face and gives me a loud, smacking kiss!

I am appalled. "Ugh! That's disgusting! I could have gotten germs!" With that Puff looks toward the audience and

Puff looks into my eyes. He is getting sleepy, very sleepy . . .

takes one paw to wipe his own mouth a couple times, which is good for another *big* laugh. Then he begins wiping his face against my tie, trying to get rid of my germs.

"Would you stop that!" I exclaim. "All right. That's it. It's time to put Puff away. He needs to get his beauty rest." I am now holding the hat to my right at eye level, about 10 to 12 inches from my face.

"Puff, look into my eyes. [Puff covers his eyes with his paws. I blow into his face and, startled, he uncovers his face.] Look into my eyes. [Puff looks at me.] You are getting sleepy, very sleepy. [Puff begins to reel, swaying around and around slightly—about a four-inch circle with my hand. The audience laughs]. *Puff, you are sleepier than that!* [A brief pause, then Puff reels broadly, swaying around and around in as large a circle as my hand can twist—about 12 inches in diameter.] More laughter.

"Go to sleep, sleep, sleep." On the third *sleep*, Puff falls

Puff the rabbit puppet sways around and around, pretending to be sleepy.

Puff says good-bye.

completely on his back with his paws pointing up. He freezes in that position. I immediately turn toward the audience and *mug*. Laughs.

"And Puff the Rabbit will stay there as long as I wish." Puff then turns his head to look at the audience as he waves to them. Then he quickly resumes his sleeping position before I catch him.

"And now, we will wake Puff up on the count of three. All together: One, two, three! Puff, wake up!" Puff does not wake up.

With concern, I say, "Puff? Puff? Are you all right?" I lean down to take a closer look at him. He quickly swings up and gives me another loud smack.

"Ugh! He got me again!" Puff wipes his face against my coat.

"Well, ladies and gentlemen, it's time to put Puff away. [Puff tries to tell me something. I let him whisper in my ear.] Puff says, 'Every puppet needs a hand,' so why don't you give him a hand now as he takes his bow." Puff bows to hearty applause.

A box of crayons . . .

. . . changes into a box of silk handkerchiefs!

Crayons to Silk

Effect

The magician displays a box of crayons. He closes the box and waves a mat or a fan in front of the crayons. When he (or she) opens the box, the crayons have vanished and a silk handkerchief is found instead.

Props Needed

(1) Gimmicked crayon box (double-sided). One side contains crayons, the other side is empty and may be loaded with a silk. You can make this crayons box yourself if you're handy with scissors and glue, or it's available for purchase from the publisher of this book.

This crayon box works on a different principle than the standard Vanishing Crayons. Our style of box enables the crayons to vanish *or* change into something else (in this case, several silks).

(2) A silk or several silk handkerchiefs.

(3) A mat or fan. Instead of the mat or fan, you could use an 8" x 10" piece of poster board.

Set-up

I use this as a quick opening effect and as a lead-in to *The Magic Knot Tube* routine using the Crystal Tube (Pavel's "Blow-knot"). It's a great way to produce the silks for any silk trick. I load three silks one at a time into the empty side of the box, then close the lid and place the crayon box on my table, with the crayon side facing up.

Routine

To show the crayons to the audience, hold the box *slightly below the center* between your thumb and middle finger. You will have to apply a little pressure to keep the box upright and prevent it from flipping over to the other side. Depending on the type of crayon box you have, the children can either see the crayons through the opening in the front of the box, or you will have to open the flap and let them see that there are crayons inside.

For pre-schoolers, I pick up the crayon box in my right hand, hold it up for display, and say, "Today I brought along a box of . . ." They finish off the sentence, "Crayons!"

I look at box in surprise. "Crayons! I thought that was oatmeal! No wonder my breakfast tasted so funny! Oh, well, I have a box of *crayons*. Now, watch them closely."

I pick up the mat with my left hand and briefly hold it in front of the crayon box. When the box is out of view—and this is something I discovered by accident one day—I can release the pressure of my thumb and middle finger and the box flips over automatically. The weight of the crayons does the trick for you!

Now I remove the mat. The crayons have only been out of sight for a few seconds. It's simply a matter of holding the mat in front of them, almost waving it by the box, just to have enough time for it to secretly flip over. When I remove the mat, the children think they are still looking at the front of a box of crayons. (And they are, it's just the *other* front!) Now I open the lid to reveal the silks. And the children gasp. Really.

The impact of Crayons to Silk is *very* strong. It's a quick, visual change, and you'll enjoy watching their surprise.

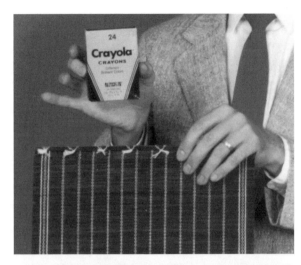

Hold crayon box between your thumb and middle finger, slightly below the middle.

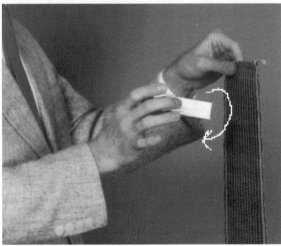

Release your grip slightly and the weight of the crayons in the top half of the box causes the box to quickly flip over. The other end of the box contains several silk handkerchiefs.

Children often will gasp or exclaim, "Look!" Even older kids—elementary age—will be impressed and surprised by the effect.

I especially like to use Crayons to Silk as an opening effect because it's quick, colorful, and visual and it fools all ages of children. When working some shows—a school with kindergarten through fifth grade or a library where pre-schoolers and elementary students are attending the same show—you have to appeal to the younger children *and* gain the respect of the older kids. Crayons appeal to the preschool children, and the strength of the effect appeals to the nine- and ten-year-olds.

Another Option

If you are performing the Magic Coloring Book, you can simply hold the coloring book in front of the crayon box for a moment instead of a mat. Then it looks as though the crayons have vanished and spread their colors throughout the coloring book. Using this option, you could omit the silks and just have the crayons vanish.

All I really need to know about how to live and what to do and how to be I learned in kindergarten. Wisdom was not at the top of the graduate-school mountain, but there in the sandpile at Sunday School.

–Robert Fulghum

Hold the coin in your left hand in full view, then drop it into your right hand.

When the coin lands in the right hand, position it in the Classic Palm. Prepare to perform the Muscle Pass by contracting your hand until the coin flips into the air back to your left hand.

More
Cash Surprises

In *Big Laughs for Little People*, I described my Miser's Dream routine, omitting two moves. I left them out to keep the description from becoming too tedious—I had already described several sleights in detail. But people who have seen me perform the complete routine or have seen it demonstrated in my lecture, have often remarked on these two features. So, here they are!

Flying Eagle
or The Muscle Pass

The Flying Eagle is accomplished with the Muscle Pass—a sleight which makes a coin appear to fall up, rather than down. This principle was first mentioned to me when I was about 15 years old by Burling Hull, who also described it in print in 1910. The concept was more fully explained by Arthur Buckley decades later and in recent years has been popularized by John Cornelius and others.

After I produce several coins from a child's head, I look at one half dollar and say, "This coin has a bird on the back. Would you like to see him fly?" Interestingly, I've never had a child say, "No—show us a card trick!"

Holding the half dollar in my left hand about 10 to 12 inches over my outstretched right hand, I say, "All right. Watch him fly . . . down." Then I drop the coin into my right hand. Some laughter and protest from the kids.

"Oh! You wanted him to fly the other way?" I position the

coin in my right hand and hold my left hand in the air, ready to catch the coin. All right, watch him fly . . . up!" I spring the coin into the air using the Muscle Pass, and catch it with my left hand. Then I pause, turn my face toward the children, with a "how about that!" expression. The children will laugh and cry out in amazement; the adults will look at each other as if to say, "Whoa! Did you see that?" This is no exaggeration. The impact of this little sleight is terrific.

Hold the coin in the Classic Palm position.

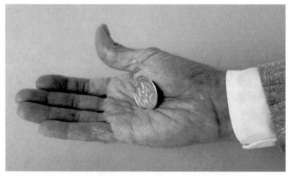

Contract your hand until you can make the coin flip over. That's the correct position. It may take another six months, but eventually you will be able to make the coin flip up into the air eight to ten inches or more.

The Ol' How-to

The effect of a coin sailing straight up into the air, without the performer making any tossing motion, is so amazing that I've even had magicians ask if I use a reel or a thread. At a convention, one man who missed my lecture asked if I would show him the Flying Eagle—someone had told him about it. I demonstrated it, and he asked if he could buy the trick! When I told him I would *give* it to him, he was excited—until I showed him how to do it!

The only gimmick in this trick is your own hand. You cause the coin to flip up out of your palm using the skin and muscles of your hand. That's all there is to it! Of course, it will take lots of practice, but it will be time well spent. Believe me when I say that you can learn it. The main reason more people don't perform this trick is not the amount of practice required: it's their lack of faith. They simply don't believe they can do it, so why waste time practicing?

So, if you don't believe you can do it, try this. Practice every day for two weeks. Begin, fully knowing that you can't learn how to do it, but you're just going to *try*. At the end of two weeks, you'll feel differently about it. You won't yet be able to do the effect as described, but you will see how much progress you can make in a relatively short period of time. With that experience under your belt, carry on—spend the next six months working on this during odd moments of the day. Then you will know how to do an amazing sleight, which can be performed anytime, anywhere, completely sur-rounded. Now, here are the specifics of *what* to practice.

The correct position for the coin is approximately the Classic Palm position. There is a certain place in your palm where you can position the coin, then contract your hand and cause the coin to turn over. Find that position. If you can make the coin turn over, you can make it fly—with time and practice, of course. The way to contract your hand is from side-to-side—bring your thumb and the left side of your hand in toward your palm until the coin is forced to turn over. At first attempt, this may seem impossible, but with a little practice you will prove to yourself that you *can* make the coin turn over.

The oldest line in the world is, "But my hand is the wrong shape." Good news: everyone's hand is the wrong shape. If this were a *natural* position and skill, everyone would be able to do it, and it wouldn't be very magical!

Keep working on it. Every day, try to get the coin to flip over. Then try to get it to flip into the air an inch or two. Keep working! After a few months of practice, you should be able to cause the coin to spring up in the air eight to ten inches. It may take you six months to reach that height, but carry on.

In performance, catch the coin in the fingers of your left hand, and be sure to display the coin immediately so the audience gets the connection: the coin was in your lower hand, now it's in your upper hand. Otherwise, the effect may be over too quickly; if they blink as the coin flies up, they may miss the point of the trick. And a trick is no good if they don't know what has happened!

A pitfall to avoid: Sometimes you see a magician burying the coin into his palm with the other hand, trying to force it into position with his left thumb. Don't do it: it looks ridiculous. Learn to find the correct position with one hand.

Also, do not make any tossing motion with your right hand. By keeping your hand still, you will create the impression that the coin flies up on its own accord.

You may find that you can attain greater height using a larger coin—perhaps a silver dollar—rather than a half dollar. I use halves because that's the size I'm comfortable with for the rest of the routine, but if you're doing this trick by itself, you may opt for the larger coin.

You can also fake the appearance of the coin going higher than it really does. Catch it in your left hand with your fingers pointing down. After you have the coin in the fingers of your left hand, rotate your hand upwards displaying it at your fingertips. Then freeze and mug. That leaves the impression—if done smoothly—that the coin ended up a few inches higher than it actually went.

The Eagle Flies Again

After the coin "falls up," I say, "Let's try that again in slow-motion. Watch close!" Here's what the audience sees: I place the half dollar in my left hand and spread my arms apart. I toss the half dollar into the air. It vanishes. While trying to follow the invisible path of the coin, it suddenly appears in my right hand.

The Sleight

Clip a half dollar (at the very edge of the coin) between the forefinger and middle finger of your right hand. Hold it up in front of you at about shoulder height to show the coin to the spectators. Your fingers should be aimed toward the spectators, as though you are pointing above their heads with your forefinger and middle finger. Since the coin is clipped between them, the face of the coin—not the edge— is facing the audience. Bring your left hand in front of the coin and pretend to take hold of the half dollar. Meantime, while the left hand conceals what your right hand is doing, swing the coin back toward your right thumb so that the half dollar is over the joint. You are still gripping the edge of the coin with your forefinger and middle finger.

Next—almost in the same motion—swing your thumb up and back, sweeping the half dollar along until it is wedged between the flesh of your thumb and the top of your hand. (At this point, your thumb has pulled the coin com- pletely loose from your fingertips. The coin is lodged behind your thumb.) As you do this, move your hands toward the right and pull away your right hand from your left. With the coin now clipped behind your right thumb, you can display

Clip the coin between the forefinger and middle finger of your right hand. Then bring your left hand up and pretend to take the coin.

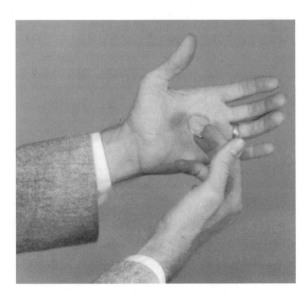

your right hand empty. (The coin should now be *dangling* behind your thumb. You can hold it with a surprisingly loose grip because the flesh at the base of your thumb and hand will keep it in place.)

Your left hand is now closed. Swing it back to your left

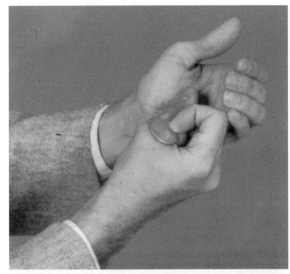

Under the cover of your left hand, swing the coin back over your thumb and let your thumb carry it behind your hand.

Close your left hand, pretending to hold the coin. It actually should be dangling from the skin behind your right thumb.

side. Your arms should now be spread apart with your right hand open, palm toward the audience, and the coin secretly clipped behind your right thumb; your left hand is closed, supposedly holding the coin.

Now pretend to toss the coin into the air. Snap the fingers of your left hand as you make the tossing motion, then immediately open your hand. The snapping noise emphasizes that something has happened and makes sure the spectators' eyes are looking at the left hand.) Leave your left hand open to show that the coin is gone. With your eyes, follow the supposed path of the coin in the air for a few seconds. Then make a small, quick upward gesture with your right hand, at the same time releasing pressure on the coin. It should slide into your right hand where you can catch it and let it slide or tumble down to your fingertips. Leave it on display in your right hand at your fingertips while you

The coin is flying through the air—invisibly. Actually, it's in the Back Thumb Palm position in my right hand.

Amazing! It landed in my other hand before any of us saw it coming!

continue looking into the air as though in search of the coin. The children will notice that the coin has now appeared in your right hand, and don't worry: they'll let you know it!

I close the trick by remarking, "The coin went a little faster than I expected!"

So, there they are—the Missing Sleights! I can't claim originality for the Muscle Pass: it goes back to the turn of the century, and probably earlier. And the Back Thumb Palm used in *The Eagle Flies Again,* is a very old sleight (though as far as I know, the particular use of this sleight and method of getting the coin there, I worked out on my own). But these old sleights give me a sense of appreciation for the magicians of days done by, and they remind me that *all* children's magic doesn't have to consist of self-working props. You can entertain them with pure sleight-of-hand.

Conclusion
(for now,
at least)

*Let
the little
children
come to me,
for of such
is the
kingdom
of God.*

–Jesus Christ

Conclusion

The word *conclusion* sounds so final, as though the end of this book were the end of the subject. But this book is certainly not the final word. In fact, I hope it's only a beginning. The Recommended Reading section to follow suggests many more books which can help expand your repertoire and develop a philosophy of entertaining the very young.

But more important than any book on the subject is the time you actually spend in front of children making them laugh. There's nothing like putting your theories to work to find out if they *do* work! The more time you spend in front of audiences, the better you will become.

After a year or so of performing full-time, I considered myself a professional. Several years later, it dawned on me that my performing skills had greatly improved. And within the last few years, I've found that I have made even more progress. I realize now that I'll always have more to learn, I will always be able to improve a patter story or work out a better arrangement of my show. After several thousand performances for children, I'm still learning. The same will be true for you. And, like me, you'll experience times of self-doubt and frustration. But if working with children is meant for you (or, I should say, if *you* are meant for working with children), the moments of frustration will be offset by the pleasure of making the little ones laugh.

While you gain experience in front of children's audiences, I hope you will keep in mind the concepts presented in *Kiddie Patter and Little Feats*. To help you remember some of them, I have singled out five key points and put them into an-easy-to-remember formula:

S

S stands for **sensitivity**. Be sensitive to the feelings of children. Pre-schoolers can be easily frightened by a loud, brusque manner. And even older, more sophisticated-appearing kids are likely to have delicate egos hidden beneath superior airs. Never insult a child of any age. Also, don't put too much pressure on a timid child on stage—giving him too many complicated tasks to perform in front of a lot of children. Be sensitive to their feelings—they'll enjoy the show more and hold you in higher esteem.

A

The next letter in the formula stands for **appropriate**: do material appropriate for the age child you're entertaining. Don't scare the little ones or baby the older kids. Sometimes people say, "What should I do when I have all ages in the same show?" I suggest omitting tricks which are too easy to figure out for older children, but if you must do a trick which is a little too simple for them, gain their allegiance. Say, "May I see your hand if you are in third grade or higher? Okay, would you close your eyes for about three minutes, because this next trick is just for the little ones. [Pause] Well . . . wait a minute. Go ahead and keep your eyes open, and maybe you can help me out with the younger kids by going along with us on this one." This lets them know that you aren't trying to fool them with, say, Farm Yard Frolics, though in fact, they may not know how it's done.

By lowering their expectations—implying that this is "an easy one," you're more likely to gain their cooperation, fool them, and still get to do something special for the pre-school and younger grades.

M

The M stands for **manual dexterity.** Do some feats which require skill. Most of the effects in *Kiddie Patter and Little Feats* are easy to perform, and there's nothing wrong with that. But stretch yourself a little: learn something a little more difficult than you think you can do. Then you'll accomplish two things.

First, you will increase your self-respect. You'll say to yourself, "I'm a better performer than I used to be." And you'll be right.

Second, you will impress the adults who are present at your children's shows. (At least you *hope* adults are going to be there!) You want the teachers or parents to leave the show saying, "Wow! That magician [or clown] was really good." You don't want them thinking, "Everything he did was so easy, he probably got it all out of a cereal box."

M

The second M is a reminder to **make** fun characters out of ordinary objects. Very young children don't care about a handkerchief. But give him a name—make him "Harry the Happy Handkerchief," and their interest is aroused. A piece of rope may not intrigue them, but if it becomes, "Sam the Skinny Snake," pre-schoolers will take more interest.

You may have noticed that I often introduce puppets and props as though they are special guest stars. "And now, let's hear a big round of applause for your friend and mine, Alice the Alligator!" or "Ladies and gentlemen, we have a famous movie star with us today . . ." Treating puppets as *more* than puppets makes them into fascinating characters.

Remember, make fun characters out of ordinary objects. In this business, it's okay to talk to a rope!

Y

Finally, Y. The show is up to **you**. You can entertain any audience, but you must tell yourself, "If it's going to be, it's up to me." It's not up to the audience to be "a good audience," it's up to you to do a good show.

Of course, there are factors which may create "a bad audience." The children may be too wound up in anticipation of Christmas. And maybe they've had five pounds of sugar— each. And their moms gave them hot dogs and Kool Aid for breakfast. And maybe the adults in the room are talking to each other instead of watching you. And none of the children have ever been disciplined or taught to respect adults. These and a hundred other factors may create unfortunate show situations.

Yet, to a large degree, you can control the reactions you receive. You can select the right material for the age group and circumstances. You can put the audience in the right frame of mind. You can adapt to the situation, rise to the occasion, and present a successful show. But always, *you must take the responsibility during the show*. Afterwards, it's all right to analyze why they may have been out of control or blasé or *whatever*. But before and during the show, "If it's going to be, it's up to me."

I hope that these five words, which create an easily remembered acrostic, will help you have more fun and be more successful in your children's shows. If it seems like a lot to remember, just be thankful I didn't use my full name!

–Samuel Patrick Smith

'Tis
the good
reader that
makes
the
good book.

–Ralph Waldo Emerson

Recommended
Reading
and
Magic

Blessed is he who, having nothing to say, abstains from giving us wordy evidence of the fact.

–George Eliot

Recommended Reading

Eldin, Peter. *The Magic Handbook* (Simon & Schuster, 1985). This is an excellent manual of classic magic. If you're an experienced performer, it's good for review and clarification. If you are just starting to perform magic for any age audience, this book can teach you the basics. Fetaque Sanders first told me about this book and gave me the copy I still have. He said, "This book is like the Tarbell Course," referring, of course, to the seven-volume magic reference books known as the *Tarbell Course in Magic*. Not all of the tricks are suitable  for a pre-school audience—the card tricks, for instance, wouldn't appeal to the very young—but many of the tricks would appeal to any age spectator.

Ginn, David. *Children Laugh Louder* (Scarlett Green Publications, 1978). Although this book isn't aimed specifically  toward pre-school children, much of the material can be adapted. David's routine for the Monster Hat is the basis of my own routine with that prop. I doubt that I would ever have tried the Monster Hat, had I not first read about it in David's book. Another good routine for pre-schoolers is *The Magic Flower* (using a simple Wilting Flower).

Ginn, David. *Comedy Warm-ups for Children's Shows* (Scarlett Green Publications, 1975). A great little book with

just the kind of nonsense pre-schoolers love! Here are ways to get them laughing and clapping and liking you early in the show.

Ginn, David. *Professional Magic for Children* (Scarlett Green Publications, 1976). This has become a standard text of children's magic. It includes a complete description of David's

Snake Can, the inspiration for my own Magic Candy Box routine. Many of the ideas in the book can be applied to entertaining pre-school children, with the obvious exception of the "element of danger" tricks. David includes a chapter on doing birthday parties which, if one is working that market, would be worth the price of the book.

Lalli, Judy. *At Least I'm Getting Better!* (Impact Publishers, 1981). A fun book of self-esteem building poems for children. You'll enjoy reading them for yourself, too.

Cooper, John. *How to Increase Your Birthday Party Business* (Published by the author, 1989). John explains a simple technique for starting your own fan club, thereby building a mailing list for birthday parties.

Lewis, Trevor. *Children's Magic Parade* (*The Linking Ring* magazine, May, 1978). Trevor Lewis is a great original thinker of children's magic. A resident of Wales, Trevor's humor plays well for American children, too.

Lewis, Trevor. *Magic for Children* (Martin Breese, Magicassettes). Not a book, but a great audio tape. Trevor's ideas seem to apply especially well to pre-school children. I particularly like his method of introducing Santa Claus at a children's Christmas party.

Lewis, Trevor. *Party Pieces* (published by the author, 1978, 1985, 1987, and 1990). The titles in this series are *Party Pieces*, *More Party Pieces*, *Further Party Pieces*, and *Still More Party Pieces*. Very clever humor and bits of business, mixed in with good children's magic.

McMahon, Greg. *Balloons on the Mailbox* (Published by the author, 1989). This little book has lots of the silliness that young children enjoy. Atlanta magician Greg McMahon explains his routines for the Pop-Away Wand, Monkey Bar, Rocky the Raccoon, Shooting a Rubber Chicken from a Cannon, and more.

McMahon, Greg. *Birthday Fun* (Published by the author, 1992). In Greg's second book of routines suitable for birthday parties and other occasions, you will find routines well-suited to pre-schoolers. One of the high-

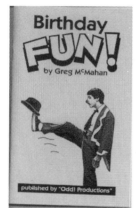

lights of the book is a section of physical comedy ideas for Rocky Raccoon (different, of course, than his *Balloons on the Mailbox* material). His advice on booking parties and packing your props is also valuable information.

Smith, Samuel Patrick. *Big Laughs for Little People* (SPS Publications, 1990). My first 200-page hardback of children's magic has many routines which can be used for pre-schoolers. (In fact, I've performed every one of the 15 routines in pre-school shows.) Especially appropriate are "Snake Cake Bake," "The Ball Brothers' Traveling Circus," and "Headband Blendo."

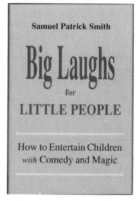

Smith, Samuel Patrick. *On Stage! Bringing Out the Better Performer in You* (SPS Publications, 1992). Entertaining pre-schoolers requires "stage skills," just as does any other venue. Your stage may be a living room or kindergarten classroom, but the principles of timing, pacing, and presentation still apply. You can read this 64-page book in one or two evenings at home and get a sound foundation in principles which are crucial to your success as an entertainer. A big promise for a little book, but read it and see!

Wagner, Karl. *Safety Magic for Children* (A Snowflake Publication, 1991.) While much of this book is geared toward elementary-age children, there are many routines which can be adapted for preschool audiences. Parents and teachers appreciate having safety messages incorporated into a show, and of course, something you say could help a child avoid an accident. That's reason enough to get this book!

Williams, Dick and Virginia. *Lights! Cameras! Magic!* (SPS Publications, 1993). For 23 years, this delightful husband and wife team appeared in their own weekly television show. This book not only tells how to do effective magic on television, it gives the methods and presentations for many of their finest routines. Much of the material is suitable for young audiences. I enjoyed the gentle humor and clever twists to their routines.

*He is
best
educated
who is
most
useful.*

–Elbert Hubbard

Recommended Magic

All of the routines in this book are appropriate for pre-school children, but this list contains additional items you may want to consider adding to your repertoire. Most of them are "dealer items"—tricks sold by magic shops and mail order magic dealers. If you are new to magic, you can often locate a nearby magic shop by looking in the yellow pages under—of all things!—Magic Shops. If you are unable to find a shop or locate a specific item, send me a self-addressed, stamped envelope for a current list of suppliers of the following items, and the other props mentioned in this book.

Samuel Patrick Smith
Post Office Box 769
Tavares, Florida 32778

(1) Bakery Bear. A cute prop made by Hank Lee's Magic Factory in Boston, Massachusetts. Similar to the old Run Rabbit Run trick. In this version, a picture of a bear vanishes. While the magician is looking for him, the bear runs across a track, from side to side, hiding behind doors. The children see the bear and tell the magician to open the door. The magician—who never sees the bear trek—opens the door but the bear is gone. He finally makes a funny reappearance.

(2) Chinese Sticks. A classic of magic, especially good for young audiences. The magician shows two magic wands, one with a long string attached to the end (with a tassel at the end of the string), and the other wand with a short string and tassel. When the magician pulls down the short string, the long string becomes short and the short string becomes long. Got it? The kids get it! They seem to like the motion of the tassels going up and down. See my routine in *Big Laughs for Little People,* entitled, "Polar Thermometers," inspired by a Fetaque Sanders routine with "Chinese Weather Sticks."

(3) Color Changing Shoelaces. Produced by David Ginn. A white shoelace, pulled through the performer's hand, turns blue. The children think the magician is hiding the white shoelace in his hand. When he finally opens his hand, there is a shoelace—but it's red! The white shoelace is found in the magician's pocket. You'll find a good routine in David Ginn's book, *Children Laugh Louder.*

(4) Crystal Tube. Made by Tenyo. An ingenious invention of Pavel, you'll find an explanation of the trick in Volume 7 of the *Tarbell Course in Magic* ("Blow-Knot," page 374), published by Louis Tannen, Inc., New York City. Three silk handkerchiefs are placed in a clear plastic tube. The magician blows them out of the tube into the air—and they are now tied together. It's a very pretty effect. Good for pre-schoolers because of the colorful silks, plus the fact that it's easy to comprehend the effect: the silks are obviously tied together. And at their tender age, just tying a knot is still a mystery! Often performed to music, I have a talking routine suitable for all ages in *Big Laughs for Little People.*

(5) The Donkey Game. Made by Supreme Magic of England. This gets a tremendous response from children. The magician tries to play Pin the Tail on the Donkey, but he can't get the tail in the right place. Then he tries to do it by magic. He vanishes the tail, but it's found on the *nose* of the donkey! He tries again, but this time the tail is no where to be found. When the magician turns around to look for it, the tail is seen dangling out from under his coat! A very funny trick, and simple to work.

(6) Fraidy Cat Rabbit. A picture of a black rabbit is shown in a little house—a simple frame with a door on the front and one on the back. When the door is opened, the rabbit is now white. He changes back and forth, but the children think the magician is turning it around. The rabbit is finally turned around so the children can see the back side. It turns out to be the back of a rabbit, as he hops away.

(7) Headband Blendo. Manufactured and sold by the author (me!). I developed this for day care center shows in 1983, and later used it in libraries, schools, and other children's shows. Five colorful headbands magically blend into a giant, multi-colored loop. In the process, there are lots of laughs trying to stop a headband from popping off of a boy's head, controlling a six-foot spring snake, and keeping track of all the headbands. Headband Blendo is available for purchase, or if you're ambitious (or know how to sew), you can make this yourself. The complete routine and explanation is in *Big Laughs for Little People.*

(8) Hoppy the Frog. Made by Supreme Magic of England. A very simple trick, but good for pre-schoolers: they like frogs, especially funny frogs. A card showing a picture of Hoppy is placed in an envelope and given to a boy. A girl on the other side of the room holds an empty envelope. The magician tries to get the frog to jump, but the girl doesn't find the frog in her envelope. Finally, exasperated, the magician pulls the card out of the boy's envelope, but Hoppy has vanished. The picture of the frog is cut out! While looking for Hoppy, the audience discovers that he is attached to the boy's back. Gets a great reaction. You'll find my routine in—of course!—*Big Laughs for Little People,* and Edwin's presentation, supplied with the trick, is very good.

(9) Instant Art. Made by Supreme Magic of England. An uncolored picture of a house is painted by magic with the help of two children from the audience. A lot of funny possibilities here in dressing up the children with smocks, berets, and handing them paint brushes, etc. At one point in my routine, I say, "Dan, a lot of great artists have worn hats. I have a hat back here which belonged to a *very* famous painter . . . Grandma Moses." And I bring out a tacky, hand-crocheted cap. "Yes," I say, "she was a great artist, but she had no taste in hats." For a complete Instant Art Routine, refer to David Ginn's *Professional Magic for Children.* If you can't find an Instant Art, the Visible Color Painting trick or the Magic Coloring Book may be substituted. In fact, some people prefer the Visible Painting.

(10) Linking Rings. A classic of magic, and one of my favorite effects. Eight large metal rings are joined and unjoined and formed into different shapes. It plays well for all ages of children. Oddly enough, this is not the very strongest effect for pre-schoolers. Perhaps they don't yet understand the impossibility of what is happening. The concept of a solid object penetrating a solid object is more impressive with elementary students. With pre-schoolers, you can get more reaction out of Hoppy the Frog! Still, it's a good stand-by and especially good when you have a mixed audience of younger and older kids. There are many booklets and articles explaining a wide variety of Linking Ring moves. A particularly good routine is found in Henry Hay's *Amateur Magician's Handbook.*

(11) Miser's Dream. Also known as Coin Catching, the magician produces money by magic, dropping half-dollars or silver dollars into a container. He pulls them from behind children's ears, which gets a great reaction. Children love this idea of the magician finding money behind their ears or under their chin. Did you ever see a grandfather (or maybe you are a grandfather) try this on his grandchild? He may have the coin palmed *very badly*, with his hand almost completely closed (known as the Advanced Grandfather Palm!), but it doesn't matter. As soon as he says, "Look, Debbie, here's a coin behind your ear" and reveals the money, the child goes berserk! My routine is in *Big Laughs for Little People.* You'll find many excellent coin moves in J.B. Bobo's *Modern Coin Magic.*

(12) Mouth Coils. Made by David Cressey and sold by many dealers. In the traditional version of the trick, the magician tears up a piece of paper, puts it in his mouth, and pulls out a 25-foot multi-colored paper streamer. This gets a great reaction from children, but in recent years, I have become hesitant to do any trick which involves putting something in my mouth or pulling it out of my mouth. Children may imitate me or their parents or teachers may consider the trick unsanitary. So, it may be better to pull the coil out of your hand instead. Just tear up a piece of paper, put it in your closed hand (which secretly contains a mouth coil), then start pulling out the coil. The colorful streamer will still create a great reaction from the children.

(13) Multiplying Billiard Balls. One ball (not really the size of a billiard ball, but about 1½ inches in diameter) becomes two balls, then three and four. If the magician is really ambitious, he can turn it into eight. This classic of magic is usually performed to music in sophisticated manipulation acts, so many magicians have mistakenly believed it can't be performed for children. To the contrary, the red balls look like part of a game, and the effect of one ball turning into two, then three, then four, is easily comprehended by young children. If you use a Surprise Finale (four-ball gimmick) for your other hand, you will get a tremendous response at the end of the trick. My routine in *Big Laughs for Little People* explains the basics and a couple of not-so-basic moves. The best over-all reference work is Burling Hull's *Expert Billiard Ball Manipulation*. Also, *The Amateur Magician's Handbook* by Henry Hay has a very good explanation of the trick.

(14) Phoney Ring. A telephone rings. The magician reaches into his coat, pulls out a phone, and begins to talk. You would think that with cordless phones, this gag would no longer be effective. But it still works, because the phone you pull out is a traditional style with a curly cord attached and evidently connected inside your coat. Using this gag, you can carry on conversations with all sorts of imaginary people. Young children like this—they've learned about the phone, it's something they know about, so it's something that interests them.

(15) Pom-pom Pole. A piece of plastic tubing has a long string on one end, a short string on the other end, and two pom-poms attached to each string. As the strings are pulled, the pom-poms move up and down, and the tube comes apart to show nothing inside. I don't usually like this trick: it seems pointless and the accompanying patter is usually inane. But Dick Williams has rescued this prop from my trash can! He created a great routine for it, where a Santa Claus doll and a Mrs. Claus doll are attached to each end of the pole. He has a great story about the "North Pole" and Mr. and Mrs. Claus' trips back and forth. You'll find it in his book, *Lights! Cameras! Magic!* which he co-authored with his wife Virginia.

(16) Pop-away Wand. Not a magic trick but a funny adjunct. A giant magic wand made of flexible plastic tubing. The ends are white caps which will pop off if you squeeze the tube. Children think this is very funny because you are out of control. You keep trying to put the ends back on the wand, but they keep popping off. Karrell Fox suggests running a piece of rope through the tube and taping or gluing the rope to the inside of each white cap. That way, the ends of the wand aren't rolling around the floor creating a temptation and distraction for the children. Trevor Lewis has some funny bits with the Pop-away Wand, described in *More Party Pieces* and *Still More Party Pieces.*

(17) Professor's Nightmare. Three pieces of rope, short, medium, and long, all become the same size. Then they are returned to their original proportions. Bob Carver and Paul Young are said to have independently originated this effect in the 1950s. There are now many versions, including very fine variations in *Amadeo's Continental Magic* and Dick and Virginia Williams' *Lights! Cameras! Magic!* Trevor Lewis has a *great* routine for this trick, found in his Hank Lee/Magic City video, *Children's Magic.* He names each rope: Stop, Look, and Listen, and ties in a very good safety message.

(18) Ring in Nest of Boxes. Another trick usually not considered "children's magic," but I've used this in hundreds of shows for little ones, and it goes over great. A borrowed ring (borrowed from a parent or teacher) vanishes when held by a boy from the audience. The magician says he will give the teacher a gift to make up for losing the ring. The gift is opened: inside is another box of a different color. When the new box is opened, inside is another box of another color. Finally, that box is opened to reveal a very small, padlocked box. The box is unlocked and inside is found the teacher's ring. A very strong effect, but get the version which uses a Lippincott Box for the finish. The method in which the last box sits behind the larger boxes creates too much of an angle problem. Kids sitting on the sides may be able to see the last box. The version using a Lippincott Box enables you to work under ordinary conditions without worrying about angles.

(19) Run Rabbit Run. See Bakery Bear, above. The same idea using a cut-out of a rabbit.

(20) Strat-O-Spheres. Three plastic balls—red, green, and yellow—are placed in a clear plastic cylinder. Magically, the red ball always ends up on bottom. Finally, the magician causes the red ball to disappear. When the tube is uncovered, the red ball is on bottom again. This is especially good for pre-schoolers because the plastic balls resemble their own toys. And you can give them funny names. "Mr. Red Head, Mr. Mellow Yellow, Mr. Green Genes" are the ones I use, suggested by North Carolina magician Steve Somers.

(21) Torn and Restored Newspaper. A newspaper is ripped to shreds, then instantly restored. Very strong magic for children or adults. You can use the funny pages for children's shows, but they even like the trick with *The Wall Street Journal*! (In fact, I've often used *The Wall Street Journal*, because every issue looks so much like previous issues, you don't have to use the same day's paper for the duplicate!) There are many versions of this trick, including the Gene Anderson method (based on Al Koran's handling) and the Shaxon method. I think Shaxon's is the finest I've seen.

Magic *Not* Recommended

This list mentions tricks which aren't appropriate or effective for pre-school audiences. Some of these may be fine for children older than, say, five. I'm not saying these are bad tricks. They are simply not the best choices for entertaining the very young.

(1) Appearing Cane (metal). I don't like to see this used in shows for very small children. Why? Such shows are usually in small quarters: a living room or a day care center.

A metal Appearing Cane can be dangerous as it springs open. Though you may have done the trick a thousand times, there is always the chance of having it open prematurely, or of having a small child plunder through your props while you're talking with the birthday mom. The plastic canes made by Fantasio would probably be fine, but I still would reserve their use for stage shows.

(2) Arm Chopper. A blade apparently penetrates someone's arm—without harming the volunteer's arm. This is absolutely too scary to small children. The same is true of the Head Chopper or guillotine illusion. This scared me when I was in second grade!

(3) Balloon Animals. Children like to see those long, skinny balloons twisted around into animal shapes. But doing this for pre-schoolers presents several problems. First, balloons are considered dangerous for young children. At an age when they put everything they find into their mouths, broken pieces of a balloon could cause a tragic accident. Some day care centers do not even allow balloons on their premises. A second problem arises when you make a balloon animal: every child wants one! The third problem comes if you succumb to pressure and actually make an animal for every child: before you finish your task, the early recipients of balloons have broken theirs and are back in line to get another one. In theory, you could stay there all day! So, my advice to those making balloon animals for children under six: don't.

(4) Bang/Flash Wand. A magic wand, loaded with caps and sometimes flash paper, makes a loud bang and flash of fire. This is simply too loud for tender tots. And fire in a pre-school show is never a good idea.

(5) Ching Soo Firecracker. A large firecracker vanishes when placed in a metal tube. It reappears on a child helper's back. While I like tricks in which a vanished object reappears on a child's back, this one is a poor choice for young kids. They are afraid of firecrackers, and rightly so. Even though there is absolutely no danger in the trick, they don't know that. So, I save this one for elementary audiences, where it brings down the house—no double-meaning intended!

(6) Dove Productions. Using any number of methods, the performer produces a live dove—from a handkerchief, dove pan, production box, etc. The reason I suggest not using dove productions for pre-schoolers is the fear factor. Young children are more timid of birds than they are of a rabbit. Doves may unexpectedly fly away, sailing over the children's heads. Rabbits rarely do that.

(7) Flash Paper. This tissue-thin paper ignites easily to create an instant, impressive flash of fire. Magicians use this in dove pans, finger flashing devices, and in other tricks. I don't encourage the use of any kind of fire in a show for young children. A magician I know was very badly burned during a birthday party show. The accident was bad enough, but it was worse that the children saw it happen.

(8) Needle Through Balloon. A long knitting needle is pushed through a balloon. The balloon doesn't pop. Finally, to prove the needle is genuine, the magician does pop the balloon. The first problem with this trick is the fear it generates. When a small child sees you with (a) an inflated balloon and (b) a large needle, what does he think? He thinks—no, he *knows*—you are going to pop that balloon. Another problem with Needle Through Balloon is that kids could try to duplicate your feat at home, causing them to handle sharp pointed objects they have no business touching.

(9) Razor Blade Trick. The performer places razor blades (or needles) into his mouth with a length of thread, then pretends to swallow. Then he pulls the blades out of his mouth, now threaded together. Although it would seem that anyone would have enough common sense *not* to do this for children, I actually saw a magician use this in a kid show! Never do anything with even the *appearance* of danger which the children could imitate.

There are hundreds of popular magic effects on the market today. You can apply the reasoning behind these examples to other tricks to see if they are appropriate.

About the Author

Samuel Patrick Smith has become well-known in the magic community through his instructional tapes, writings and seminars for magicians. I am pleased to write a few words about Sammy, because he has been an inspiration to me, and, I'm happy to add, a good friend.

I first became acquainted with Sammy when I purchased his two audio-cassette tape albums, *Booking Yourself* and *Make It Happen*. These cassettes offered sound suggestions on establishing a magic business, and also served to inspire me when I found myself discouraged with my perceived lack of progress.

Sammy and I met at an Abbott's Get-together in 1988, and we corresponded over the course of a few months. Then a Florida vacation offered my wife, Brenda, and I the opportunity to visit him at his home in Tavares. We were thrilled when he offered us the chance to attend one of his day care shows the next morning.

I remember thinking, "I know Sammy's excellent at managing the business end of magic, but how well can he perform?" My question was answered within the first few minutes of his show. It was, quite simply, one of the best children's shows I had ever seen.

It's hard to describe in print, but there was a happy, magical feeling in the air that morning. I could tell that Sammy really cared about the children, and they loved him right back. The pre-school director I spoke with couldn't say enough good things about Sammy and the numerous shows he had presented there over the years. Just hearing her comments made me feel proud to be a magician, too!

Since that morning in 1989, I have become a better kid-show performer, thanks in large part to Sammy. I have seen him work at several pre-schools, always with great success, and his performances always inspire *me* to do a better job. Some of my best kid show routines are adapted from his first book of magic for children, *Big Laughs for Little People.*

I have been fortunate to see Sammy perform most of the routines in this new book. Any one of them will be a big hit with your younger audiences. They've worked for him, they've worked for me. I know they'll work for you!

—Martin Hahne